SONNETS

Image credits:

FRONT: Said to be of Christoph Friedrich "Fritz" Heinle, Göttingen, 1912.
Walter Benjamin Archive
P. 209, Kenneth Mroczek
P. 233, 235, Walter Benjamin Archive
All others Carl Skoggard

Published in the United States by Fence Books
Science Library, 320
University at Albany
1400 Washington Avenue
Albany, NY 12222

www.fenceportal.org

This book was printed by Versa Press
and distributed by Small Press Distribution
and Consortium Book Sales and Distribution.

Library of Congress Control Number: 2017949980

ISBN 13: 978-1-9443800-1-4

FIRST EDITION

10 9 8 7 6 5 4 3 2

SONNETS

WALTER BENJAMIN

TRANSLATION, INTRODUCTION, AND
COMMENTARY   CARL SKOGGARD

FOREWORD   MEGAN EWING
AFTERWORD   CHRISTIAN WOLLIN

FENCE BOOKS

Albany New York

CONTENTS

FOREWORD

MEGAN EWING

CAPRICIOUS MOSAICS:
BENJAMIN'S SONNETS AND THE WORK OF MOURNING

Walter Benjamin's sonnets leave us with the question of their relevance for a large, multifaceted body of critical work. Those familiar with his oeuvre will hardly be surprised that some of his earliest writings experimented intensively with poetic form. Certainly, his critical prose is some of the most complex and image-driven in the modern German canon. Are these seventy-three Petrarchan sonnets to be regarded as early works that offer insight into Benjamin's "conversion" to literature[1] in evidence in his first major literary essay, "Two Poems by Friedrich Hölderlin" (1914–15)[2], or

---

1   See Michael W. Jennings, "Benjamin as a Reader of Hölderlin: The Origins of Benjamin's Theory of Literary Criticism," *The German Quarterly* 56, No. 4 (Nov., 1983), pp. 544–62, here p. 545.

2   As noted in an essay on Stefan George, Benjamin wrote "Two Poems by Hölderlin" in dedication to Fritz Heinle, the mourned subject of the sonnets: "In early 1914 [George's] Stern des Bundes [the poetic cycle "The Star of the Covenent"] rose, and a few months later, the war came....My friend [Heinle] died. Not in battle....Months followed....In these

to be recuperated as innovative stand-alone works?

The sonnets' passionate fixation on the figure of Fritz Heinle has made them easier to dismiss as juvenilia, a youthful homoerotic attraction largely sublated as worship for Heinle's poetic talent. But read as a paratext to the Hölderlin essay, the sonnets reflect the early development of epistemological and aesthetic positions that Benjamin maintained throughout his life as a writer. As translator Carl Skoggard tells us, he takes Benjamin's enjoinder from "The Task of the Translator" to heart in his rendering of these poems:

> For what does a literary work 'say'? What does it communicate? It 'tells' very little to those who understand it. Its essential quality is not communication or the imparting of information.[3]

Skoggard's sonnets maintain the loftiness of Benjamin's expression, the hermeticism he adopts as a reader of the sprung syntax of Hölderlin's late hymns, and the ensuing mystery and vigor of the sonnets' images while freeing the work from the original's straitjacketed end rhyme. Most importantly, his translation makes palpable the deadly seriousness with which

---

months, however (which I devoted entirely to my first work of some scope — an essay on two poems of Hölderlin, which was dedicated to my friend) — the poems he was able to leave behind came to occupy the few places in my being where poems could still have a decisive effect on me [*wo noch in mir Gedichte bestimmend zu wirken vermochten*]." As quoted in Stanley Corngold, "Benjamin's 'Affective Understanding'," *Complex Pleasure: Forms of Feeling in German Literature* (Stanford: Stanford UP, 1998), pp. 150–170, here p. 153.

3   Walter Benjamin, "The Task of the Translator," *Selected Writings Volume 1 — 1913–1926*, eds. Marcus Bullock and Michael W. Jennings (Cambridge: Harvard/Belknap, 1996) pp. 253–63, here p. 253.

Benjamin approaches the poetic endeavor of the sonnets. If we are to understand the significance of these poems and the figure of Fritz Heinle whom they mourn and address for Benjamin's formation as critic-philosopher,[4] we must turn to his incipient understanding of the poet's activity for the larger metaphysical phenomenon he terms "poetic destiny."[5] This is a notion borrowed from Hölderlin and transformed into something uniquely Benjaminian in the "Two Poems" essay.

Both Hölderlin and the essay itself remained central points of reference for Benjamin throughout his career. Writing in 1930, he referred to the essay as one of the "grand foundations" of his thought.[6] Hölderlin was regarded in Benjamin's literary milieu as "one of the supreme figures in poetry" at the time of the essay's composition.[7] While "Two Poems" was dedicated privately to Heinle, it is Gershom Scholem's recollections that make an identification of Heinle and Hölderlin indisputable: "Benjamin

---

4   Benjamin is neither purely a philosopher nor a literary critic; as Gershom Scholem noted, each of his literary essays lays out a philosophy of its object.

5   Benjamin, "Two Poems by Friedrich Hölderlin," *Selected Writings Volume 1 — 1913–1926*, eds. Marcus Bullock and Michael W. Jennings (Cambridge: Harvard/Belknap, 1996), pp. 19–36, here p. 25

6   From a letter to Scholem dated April 26, 1930. Walter Benjamin, *Gesammelte Briefe III*, p. 521, trans. mine.

7   Friedrich Hölderlin was rediscovered by literary scholar Norbert von Hellingrath, who in 1909 found the 19th-century poet's Pindar translations in the Stuttgart Library and subsequently began the project of publishing his complete works. Stefan George and his circle became devotees after von Hellingrath passed on the Pindar translations through Karl Wolfskehl, a member of George's group. George's endorsement and von Hellingrath's editions of the complete works ensured Hölderlin's influence upon an entire generation of young German academics that included not only Benjamin, but such figures as Martin Heidegger, Klaus Mann, and Carl Schmitt.

perceived his deceased friend, whom Ludwig Strauss later described to me as 'a wholly lyric poet,' as a figure akin to Hölderlin."[8] Lacking access as we do to Heinle's full body of work, the sonnets that mourn him offer a direct connection to his arguably considerable influence upon Benjamin's early poetological thought.

Hölderlin's own writings evince a belief in the poem as both a means of producing, *and* the instantiation of knowledge, an idea that underwrites Benjamin's own conception of the value of the art object for his subsequent writings. Hölderlin resists Kant's assertion that the noumenal or transcendental realm is wholly inaccessible to us. He instead understands the poet's unique activity as a means to render the transcendental perceptible. The poet's activity is the attempt, modeled on religious experience, to attain to this realm, in order to bring some knowledge of it to his people, regardless of personal cost. This Promethean activity is conceived, in other terms, as an attempt to span the subject-object divide, a gulf framed as fundamentally unbridgeable in Kant's philosophy. In "Two Poems by Friedrich Hölderlin," Benjamin insists on Hölderlin's claim to the attainability of such unity *through the act of writing*: in the activity of poetry itself, the cognition of something beyond it is made possible. Poetic inspiration renders the presence of the divine or transcendent palpable [*fühlbar*] for Hölderlin, and it is this revelatory power of the poem that captures Benjamin's attention. It is a view that will inflect his writing for the remainder of his career—a turn of thought whereby the work of art comes to function as a vessel for "absolute truth in a fallen world" that underwrites Benjamin's con-

---

8   Gershom Scholem, *Walter Benjamin: The Story of a Friendship* (New York: Schocken, 1981), p. 17.

version to literature invoked above.[9] He writes, "The gods and the living are bound together in the destiny of the poet by ties of iron." The passage continues:

> It is said of the poem, which leads men "toward return-ing, ingathering, homecoming" [*der Einkehr zu*], that it leads them "like the heavenly one" [*Himmlischen gleich*]— and leads the heavenly ones themselves. The actual basis of the comparison is transcended, for the continuation says that the poem leads the heavenly ones, too, and no differently from men. Here, at the center of the poem, the orders of gods and men are curiously raised up toward and against each other, the one balanced by the other. (Like two scales: they are left in their opposing positions, yet lifted off the scale beam.)[10]

To flesh out the grounds upon which the poem comes to contain Truth, Benjamin here argues for the coincident movement of both the transcen-dental and phenomenal toward their opposites in the activity of poetry. The moment of unity is achieved as the divine assumes a concrete form—as the sensible realm comes to host transcendental force in the form of the poem itself—while simultaneously the concrete and sensible are elevated to the level of the idea. In the instance of Hölderlin's "Timidity," one of the two poems under examination in the essay, humans ("the people" or "the living") become members of a new "order," losing their identity and phys-ical bodies to assume significance as a symbol, Benjamin argues, of poetry

---

9   Jennings, "Benjamin as a Reader," p. 545.
10 Benjamin, "Two Poems," pp. 24–25.

itself. Where Hölderlin contended in his writings that the divine could be made merely palpable for the reader by the activity of the poet, Benjamin's radicalization of this claim is an insistence on the transformation of the transcendental into the phenomenal: the total interpenetration of spirit and matter. The "poet's destiny" is then to act as the medium (the means or "middle" itself, however — not as a mediator maintaining an individual subjectivity with its unique claims to experience) for these intertwined transformations, and the poem, as the container of the knowledge thus produced. Sonnet 55 undergirds this understanding of Hölderlin's influence, specifically upon the manner in which truth is contained in literature:

> I am painter who from shadows
> Paints a most astounding likeness
> And dearer for him are his colors
> Than for others theirs so rich and full
>
> When no one longer boasts of theirs
> Still shall my dull tints glow
> As old mosaics send forth rays
> Above grave markers squat and low

In Benjamin's interpretation of "Timidity," the relationship, created by the activity of poetry, of the poet to his people is metaphorized as a mosaic: "Now, depersonalized, the people appears (may we compare this with Byzantine mosaics?) as if pressed in the surface around the great flat figure of its sacred poet."[11] This metaphor of the mosaic is directly linked,

---

11   Benjamin, "Two Poems," p.28.

as Michael Jennings has shown, to Benjamin's treatment of epistemological problems in the preface to *The Origin of the German Mourning Play* (1925), in which ideas are described as constellations, "capricious mosaics" of truth fragments. The mosaic of the sonnets proposes the art object as an enduring source of the light of truth, but one refracted by the fragmentary shards it comprises. Its presence further underscores the fact that Benjamin's category of fragmentation was already in development well before his engagement with Jewish mysticism.

Into the 1930s, Benjamin continued to rely on this notion that the work of art, and literature in particular, contains such truth fragments accessible to us in the phenomenal world. While "Two Poems by Friedrich Hölderlin" does not evince Benjamin's mature position on the truth content of the work of art later laid out in the 1924 article on Goethe's *Elective Affinities* (in which such content is the concern of critique [*Kritik*] rather than literary commentary), the earlier essay proposes a role for the commentator-critic that elevates him to the level of the poet in producing knowledge. The work of the sonnets, the work of mourning, is a complementary undertaking that aspires to the production of truth content through the poetological processing of the life, work, and most significantly, death of Fritz Heinle. Benjamin assumes with some trepidation the mantle of poet-medium, hypostatizing what is now beyond (Heinle),[12] while simultaneously elevating the sensible, phenomenal figure of his friend to the level of symbol — specifically that of "sacred poet" and teacher of the courage particular to that office. Sonnet 63 registers Benjamin's own position as the disciple (a member of a "troop" of "thy faithful ones") and hermetic

---

12   Scholem noted, "As was evident from Benjamin's every reference to Heinle, death had moved his friend to the realm of the sacrosanct," *Walter Benjamin*, p. 17.

chronicler of a now Christ-like Heinle: "I have made the wooing and the fearing / Of those highest days a lasting part of me / And stayed behind the writer of thy deeds." Sonnets 7 and 8 depict a reciprocal inscription of the poet and his transcendental object, representatives of the orders of god and men bending toward one another in the activity of poetry. In 7, the poet is inscribed: "All the while the teaching word thy finger etches / On the tablet of my thought." In 8, the transcendent principle is marked by the poet: "In thy body is my loving chiseled." These lines describe a perfect interpenetration of spirit and matter through a symmetrical inversion of inscribed parts and the forces of inscription. In the first, Heinle's "finger," a notably embodied metaphor for a transcendental force, etches the hard stuff of the poet's mind. In the second, it is Heinle's figurative "body" that is chiseled by the poet's incorporeal Love.

In Sonnet 3, Benjamin attributes his spiritual-intellectual birth to Heinle, again made to function as an exalted, generative force: "Thou blessed Birth how deeply silent I / arose from him was in that hour made." While Skoggard translates the German *bestimmt* as "made" in order to convey the utter definition Benjamin intends and maintain rhythmic coherence, the word is most often understood as "determined." Such neo-Kantian determination forms the focus of the Hölderlin essay. The essay defines the "poetic task" as the "preliminary condition of an evaluation of the poem," which

[...] cannot be guided by the way the poet has fulfilled his task; rather the seriousness and greatness of the task itself determine the evaluation. For the task is derived from the poem itself. The task is also to be understood as the precondition of the poem, as the intellectual-perceptual [*geistig-anschaulich*] structure of the world to which the poem bears witness [...] Nothing will be said here about the process of lyrical composition, nothing about the person or world view of the creator; rather, the particular and unique sphere in which the task and precondition of the poem lie will be addressed."[13]

What Benjamin proposes here as a unique sphere he will develop as "the poetized" [*das Gedichtete*] — an "inner form" that preexists the poem itself and determines its expression. It is also circularly conceived as the product of the task, thus doing away with a form-content model of aesthetic critique: "instead of separating [form and content], it distinctively stamps in itself their immanent, necessary connection."[14] The poetized is the essence out of which poems are made, that which defines the task of their creator (one permeated with the possibility of failure, as any single poem invariably fails to perfectly fulfill its task) *and* that task's product. Returning to the example of Sonnet 8 above, the second image makes manifest this aspect of the poetized, insofar as the poet's love is at once precondition, the agent of inscription and its aesthetic product: Love chisels itself into the body, and thus remains present to it as its own trace.

Under the sign of the poetized, the sonnets, aesthetically imperfect as Benjamin knew them to be, would yet have been evaluable as containing some fragmentary coherences between their precondition of loss and mourning that defined the poetic task and the produced poems, which speak of their lost object in the language of religious experience.[15]

---

13   Benjamin, "Two Poems," p. 18.

14   Ibid., p. 19.

15   Another early essay of Benjamin's from 1912, "Dialogue on the Religiosity of the Present" shares with Hölderlin's "On Religion" the view that man should base his experience of the sensible on religious revelation.

Skoggard renders the Du-form of divine address with the English "Thou" to good effect. For the young writer's purposes, this language is not only suited to the capture of the complex and profound affects and insights of loss, but also underscores the transcendental status of the addressed figure, whose self-determined surrender to death becomes for the early Benjamin the mark of the sacred poet.

In his evaluation of Hölderlin's two poems, Benjamin takes stock of the shifts between them, valorizing with increasing force the merits of the later "Timidity" over the incoherences with regard to the poetized that characterize the early version, "The Poet's Courage." Hölderlin's subject is the nature of poetic courage, and the poetized of the poems Benjamin concludes "is the supreme sovereignty of relationship,"

> shaped in this particular poem as courage — as the innermost identity of the poet with the world, whose emanation is all the identities of the perceptual and the intellectual in this poem. That is the basis on which the isolated figure is repeatedly transcended in the spatiotemporal order, where it is sublated as formless, polymorphous, event and existence, temporal plasticity and spatial happening. All known relations are united in death, which is the poet's world. In death is the highest infinite form and formlessness, temporal plasticity and spatial existence, idea and sensuousness.

Courage is then the wholesale "surrender [of the poet] to relationship," to his identity as creator in a world "saturated with danger."[16] Sonnet 66

---

16   Benjamin, "Two Poems," p. 34.

reflects these judgments in proclaiming the day of his poetic birth "full of danger full of blood." The poetized of the sonnets as I read them is Benjamin's own exploratory surrender to relationship, to his relation of worship — intellectual, spiritual, and otherwise of Heinle's memory and death. In "The Poet's Courage," the titular courage is conceived according to Benjamin as a mere quality, whereas in the mature poem this willingness to surrender "becomes less a quality than a relation of man to world and of world to man." This immanent relation he believes, as the sonnets evidence, the poet Heinle grasped, like Hölderlin before him. The poet faces death no longer as force utterly apart from himself, whose danger is to be withstood and overcome with beauty. Instead, beauty "flows from the overcoming of danger." Benjamin seems to be speaking directly to Heinle's suicide when he continues, "Courage is submission to the danger that threatens the world. It conceals a peculiar paradox [...] the danger exists for the courageous person, yet he does not heed it. For he would be a coward if he heeded it; and if it did not exist for him, he would not be courageous. This strange relation dissolves, in that the danger threatens not the courageous one himself but rather the world. Courage is the life-feeling of the man who surrenders himself to danger, so that in his death he expands that danger into a danger for the world and at the same time overcomes it."[17] In such a death, as Heinle's was for Benjamin, and perhaps as he conceived his own twenty-five years later in Portbou, Spain, the poet-critic claims a certain triumph. Sonnet 63 announces for us, his devoted readers: "Accept the slender palm of costly victory / From thy faithful ones who saw thee go / And didst no further show thyself among us."

---

17   Ibid., p. 33.

INTRODUCTION

CARL SKOGGARD

WALTER BENJAMIN AND HIS SONNETS OF MOURNING

That Walter Benjamin wrote an extensive series of sonnets to mourn the death of Christoph Friedrich Heinle, a promising poet who took his own life at the age of 20, days after the First World War had begun, is not widely known. Benjamin worked on these sonnets for a long time, possibly a decade. Now and then he would read from them to his household circle; in 1923 he thought to send samples to Florens Christian Rang, a distinguished older man with whom he had come to be on excellent terms and who might have passed them on to a prospective publisher. But the poems appear to have stayed with Benjamin. They were among the writings he eventually entrusted to Georges Bataille in 1940 for safekeeping, when continuing in France was impossible. Publication would wait until forty-six years after Benjamin's death; the present translation makes them available to readers of English for the first time.[1]

    Benjamin the writer of sonnets seems to raise a special problem for his admirers. Even today, the fact that they are the central undertaking of his early adult years has not registered in the literature. Perhaps this is because people cannot bring themselves to consider Benjamin as a poet, or cannot conceive of his having turned to the writing of poetry to confront crucial issues in his life. Defining Benjamin has never been easy. Indeed, during the years he was producing his sonnets, young Benjamin was also imagining that he would be the next to advance German metaphysics. As well, he saw himself becoming the leading critic of German literature. In the end, however, despite highly original contributions to both fields, Benjamin would not bequeath anything like a life's work to either.[2]

As Hannah Arendt pointed out in her seminal essay, whatever Benjamin left for posterity was altogether *sui generis*. Nothing he did resembled what had been written by others before him or was likely to be repeated, least of all by himself. Moreover, Benjamin was in everything he touched an amateur:

> His erudition was great, but he was no scholar; his subject matter comprised texts and their interpretation, but he was no philologist; he was greatly attracted not by religion but by theology and the theological type of interpretation for which the text itself is sacred, but he was no theologian and not particularly interested in the Bible; he was a born writer, but his greatest ambition was to produce a work consisting entirely of quotations.

This list concludes with the observation that Benjamin "thought poetically, but he was neither a poet nor a philosopher."[3]

Certainly Benjamin's sonnets are unlike any others. Arendt, a friend to Benjamin during his last Paris years, may not have known of them. Few people were ever informed of the project; fewer still were shown poems. During the years he was actively at work on the sonnets, only Gershom Scholem, who was his closest associate and heard Benjamin read some of them, was fully initiated and could sense their great importance for him.[4] To a large extent, therefore, their limited reception must be laid at the door of Benjamin himself, always inclined to secrecy about what he cared for most. Subsequent to Benjamin's death, those who had known him best simply assumed that certain sonnets dedicated to a deceased friend of his early youth were among his lost works. The sonnets would be rediscovered in Paris, in the Bibliothèque nationale, in 1981. But so far their unearthing has not granted them a firm place in anyone's understanding of Benjamin and his work.[5]

In turning to sonnets, Benjamin took care to heed traditional formal patterns. In his hands, however, respect for convention only contributes to an essential strangeness. The strangeness begins with the simple fact that he would spend years producing so many of them — seventy-three in total — for a dead (male) friend. But in the desolation of the First World War, writing sonnets became for him a secret obsession. These were otherworldly sonnets in which Benjamin looks to a far-off constellation of unchanging metaphysical reality for consolation. They have nothing to do with the vicissitudes of a love relationship in the here and now, as Shakespeare's do — though like his predecessor, Benjamin is a poet-lover seeking special favor. That favor will be rarified spiritual communion with the friend, achieved through the very process of mourning him. At the same time, Benjamin's sonnets are his idiosyncratic response to the conflict around him, about which he was largely silent otherwise.[6]

Apart from what one gleans from the poems, evidence of the relationship between Benjamin and "Fritz" Heinle comes chiefly from letters

Benjamin penned during the spring and summer of 1913, and from the *Berlin Chronicle*, a memoir of his early years in Berlin written shortly before Benjamin left Germany for good — that is, nearly two decades after the events being recalled.[7] The letters, filled with youthful élan, let us trace the beginnings of a powerful attraction of opposites between the twenty-year-old Benjamin and an unconstrained and impetuous Rhinelander not quite two years his junior.[8] Their meeting took place in the picturesque subalpine town of Freiburg im Breisgau, where both had enrolled in the university. Within weeks they were hiking together in the surrounding mountains and drinking together in taverns. Benjamin's missives, addressed to former schoolmates in Berlin, show that almost immediately he sought to have Heinle's poetry published — efforts proving fruitless then and later.[9] The most interesting of Benjamin's comments indicate that he, Benjamin, so highly reserved and intensely intellectual, was falling under the sway of his new friend.

Heinle is first mentioned in a positively chatty communication dated 29 April 1913 which Benjamin addressed to Herbert Blumenthal (later Belmore):

> And look at the sort of people I associate with! You will be hearing about this also from Sachs. There is Keller, who has the beginning of a new novel that is significant; he has a pretty girlfriend whom I often see. There is Heinle, a good young fellow. "Tipples and eats hearty and makes poems." They are supposed to be very nice. I'll soon be hearing a few. Forever dreaming and German. Not well-dressed.

Franz Sachs was another Berlin school friend. The letter continues: "Take note, I go around only with Christians here, and please tell me what that means." Nearly all the letters surviving from this period of Benjamin's life were addressed to Jewish peers from his own assimilated Berlin background.[10]

The Freiburg letters routinely refer to Heinle. One to Sachs (4 June 1913) shows Benjamin already intent on having "odes" by Heinle published. Another to Blumenthal dated June 7 contains Heinle's "latest": *Portrait*. With six musical lines of rhyming iambic pentameter, the poem seizes on a moment of erotic surrender:

> From yellow linen rises tan and clear
> The slender neck upright. Yet full aware
> Of feasts bestowed down sinks the singéd pair
> In handsome arcs to cambered pleasure.
> Like dark grapes spring the pair of lips
> With sudden ripeness to the heaving breast.[11]

By July 3, Benjamin can speak of Heinle and himself to Blumenthal as a pair of friends detached from the rest:

> Heinle has turned out to be the only student with whom I continue to be on truly personal terms. Keller is now neurasthenic....Lately I was witness to a frightfully embarrassing scene....The fact that Heinle and I had nothing whatsoever to do with it — but were seen by both parties as uninvolved, should provide you with the evidence of our defined and thoroughly isolated position.

The same letter lays bare the closeness which was developing between these two and how Benjamin nevertheless suffered from loneliness:

> Recently I made the acquaintance of a female student from Essen, whose name is Benjamin. We took a walk on the Schönberg,...one of the fairest peaks I know. I want to go there at night some time with Heinle. We talk of many things easily and gaily—each time when I think of this walk, it comes to me how greatly I lack for people here. Heinle is really the only one.

Some of the last mentions of Heinle from Freiburg are in his defense, against criticism that had been directed against both his prose and his poetry. Now Benjamin concedes that Heinle expresses himself from the heart rather than through ideas (letter to Sachs, July 11) and that a certain poem of his is "hard to understand and not perfect" (to Blumenthal, July 17). Most revealing is the confession to Blumenthal which follows: "Here [in Freiburg] we are perhaps more aggressive, more vehement, and less inclined to reflect (literally!). What I really mean is: he *is* so and I feel it after him, with him, and am often so myself."

That autumn the young men migrated to Berlin to attend university there. But now enthusiasm for Heinle's poetry is no longer a feature of Benjamin's correspondence. Instead his references, for the most part in passing, have to do with their frenzied activities within the "youth culture movement," or Jugendkulturbewegung. Already in Freiburg both had been active in this movement, through which university students were beginning to ask for more say in their education and development, and to advocate on behalf of others still younger than themselves. The more radical students envisioned a fully autonomous youth culture which would usher in the regeneration of Wilhelmine society as a whole. And though it was always a tame affair (violence was never threatened), the Jugendkulturbewegung alarmed conservatives. Every month its journalistic organ, *Der Anfang*, issued a summons to youth: to create itself, to harness that yearning for an ideal which belonged to it alone — and to resist being molded for the existing order through the patriarchal family, schools and universities, and the church.[12]

Along with his friend Heinle, Benjamin soon assumed a prominent role in the student leadership in Berlin. The Jugendkulturbewegung, however, was prey to infighting; and eventually Benjamin and Heinle, too, found themselves at odds. One of Benjamin's letters of the time contains his gravely beautiful account of the quarrel which briefly interrupted their friendship:

> Yesterday evening Heinle and I found ourselves together on the way to Bellevue station. We spoke only of meaningless things. Then all at once he said: "Actually, I should really have a great deal to say to you." Whereupon I invited him to go right ahead, that it was high time. And since he really did want to tell me something, I was eager to hear it and at his urging went with him to his room.
>
> At first we went over and over what had happened, trying to explain, and so forth. But soon we felt what it was about, and said as much: That it was very hard for the two of us to separate from each other. And I realized one thing that was the important aspect of this discussion, namely, that he knew perfectly well what he had done, or

rather, it was no longer for him a matter of "knowing," so definite and necessary did he really view our opposition to each other, just as I had expected he would. He placed himself over and against me in the name of Love, and I countered with the Symbol. You understand the simplicity and the richness of the friendship for us, how for us it contains both these things. The moment came when we confessed that we were up against fate: we said to each other that each could be in the other's place.

With this discussion, which I am scarcely able to relay to you in this letter, we each withstood the sweetest temptation. He withstood the temptation of emnity, and offered me friendship, or at least brotherliness, from then on. I withstood by rejecting — you do see — what I could not accept.

Sometimes I have thought that we two, Heinle and I, understand each other the best among all the people we know. But this is not quite right. Rather: Even though we are each other, each must of necessity stay true to his own spirit [*Geist*].[13]

The remainder of the letter confirms that tensions between the friends had grown out of differences within the youth culture movement. Yet the specifics of their quarrel are hard to discern. How it was resolved sounds cryptic, too, in Benjamin's telling, found in his *Berlin Chronicle* (notice 12): "Even now I am able to recall the smile which made up for all the dreadfulness of the weeks of our separation, and with which he [Heinle] made what seemed an almost irrelevant mention of a magic formula, healing the injured party [Benjamin]."

Then, abruptly, war came and the "youth culture movement" was deprived of relevance. Most young men who were Benjamin's age rushed to arms. But during the night of August 8, 1914, Fritz Heinle, deciding otherwise, ended his life. With him was his lover, Rika Seligson. The *Berlin Chronicle* relates that on the following morning Benjamin awoke to an express letter from his friend containing the words: "You will find us lying in the Heim." The "Heim" was a meeting place for students belonging to the group led by Benjamin; here the two had used kitchen gas to asphyxiate themselves. Various local papers of the day were satisfied that the couple had been unhappy in love.[15] Persons closest to them knew more.

The *Berlin Chronicle* also speaks of the confusion and excitement of the first days of the conflict. Benjamin and other members of his circle had "huddled together" in the Café des Westens on Berlin's Kurfürstendamm to choose which garrison they might apply to as a group. "My place, too, was among the surge of bodies then swelling in front of the garrison gates," Benjamin would recall,

> no matter how reserved my thinking, according to which one's sole course could be to secure a place among friends in the unavoidable call-up. Admittedly this was only for two days: On the eighth the event intervened which caused this city and this war to sink from my sight for a long time.[16]

In the aftermath of the suicides, rather than volunteer to become a soldier, Benjamin obtained the first of several military deferments. And he did not hesitate before resigning his post as student leader.[17] In the summer of 1915 he left Berlin for Munich, where he no longer involved himself in politics of any sort and did not care to discuss the war, whether in corre-spondence or in conversation.[18] Nor would he discuss the disappearance of his friend. In 1917 he decamped for Switzerland; not until 1920 did he return to live in Germany.

The most illuminating of Benjamin's comments from after the start of the war, which he addressed to a fellow student leader, concerns the sud-den demise of the youth movement:

> The youth movement I see as ended with this war. Not through this war, but through the youth. "With" this war because it only required failure in the face of this occur-rence to show that there really is none [i.e., no "youth" in Benjamin's idealizing collective sense]. Yet things are not hopeless. It simply means: Youth as well is too great a detour on the path to realization of Spirit [*Geist*].[19]

Benjamin reacted to the war and the double suicide as to a single trau-matic event. Together they would create the hinge of his before and after. Heinle's death would be the first and the supreme sacrifice of the war — tantamount to the death of Youth itself.[20] Precisely when Benjamin began to mourn his friend in sonnets is uncertain; no dates are immedi-ately associated with the manuscripts which preserve them. The evidence of handwriting, paper types, and ink makes it probable, however, that this was shortly after the outbreak of hostilities. Most of his work would be accomplished before the war ended.[21]

Some idea of what Benjamin was feeling and thinking is gained from his first ambitious essay, *Zwei Gedichte von Friedrich Hölderlin* [Two Poems by Friedrich Hölderlin], written during the winter of 1914–15. It deals with dangers facing "the poet." Mustering scholastic detachment, Benjamin compares two versions of a Hölderlin poem.[22] He appears to want to show how the poet-figure in the earlier of them, burdened by a fearful sense of mission, one for which he might lose his own life, in the second enters a new cosmic order where his individuality is absorbed into a dense and intimate network of divine and human forces sustaining him and, at the same time, sustaining the order which he, the poet, helps uphold through the act of writing the poem before us. Or so Benjamin seems to be saying, but his difficult essay does not directly bring up war any more than do Hölderlin's poems, contemporary with the wars of Napoleon.

Many years later, writing to commemorate the 60th birthday of another poet, the celebrated Stefan George, Benjamin recalled Fritz Heinle:

> Early in 1914 the *Stern des Bundes* [a collection of poems by George] rose fatefully above the horizon, and a few months later there was war. Before the hundredth man had fallen, it broke into our midst. My friend died. Not in battle. He bled on the field of honor where one does not "fall." Months ensued of which I recall nothing. In these months, however — which I devoted entirely to my first larger study, an essay on two poems by Hölderlin, which was dedicated to him, my friend — it happened that what he had left behind in the way of poems came to occupy those few regions within me where poems could still exercise any power. They created a different figure.

That figure is, of course, the same as "the poet" in Benjamin's Hölderlin essay.[23]

The sonnets which Benjamin was starting to write are also concerned with a poet. He has died, leaving behind a mourner who now turns poet himself to perform his mourning. That a grieving person might wish to borrow the characteristics and properties of the deceased, we readily understand; the griever may begin wearing clothes which belonged to the other, or suddenly it may be apparent that he has come to embody the other's defining mannerisms. Such appropriations of personality in particular strike us as uncanny — rather like the performances of a sleepwalker. Benjamin, however, having assumed the role of his friend, that of poet, remains self-aware. It is a role he mentions from within the sonnets as if he were a character — now invoking sonnet writing as his way to memorialize the deceased and again as his own penance, now measuring the extent to which poetizing is a remedy for his suffering and then, again, seeing in it the means for uniting himself with the friend.[24]

Benjamin's poems do not imitate those of Heinle, and as a body of work, outweigh the known poems by Heinle. As previously remarked, his sonnets are unlike the sonnets written by anyone else. Equally remote from dramatic utterance and from sustained lyricism, they strike us as the expression of some hermetic *thought process*. Feeling states are never appealed to as such but emerge from complex mental refraction. Benjamin's labor of mourning advances, but only in step with his exploration of a private metaphysical terrain. Repeated images in his sonnets suggest a conceptual system never openly declared; puzzling allusions are scattered everywhere. Those traits — taken with his diction, a mingling of the sober, the odd, and the lofty, and literal treatment of sonnet form and peculiar syntax, to be examined later — create what Benjamin might have called his "physiognomy" as a sonneteer. They constitute a recognizably Benjaminian poetics.[25]

To serve as an epigraph for his manuscript collection of fifty of the sonnets, Benjamin carefully copied out a stanza from Friedrich Hölderlin's hymn *Patmos*. Its lines lament the loss of one "upon whom beauty did most / Hang" and deplore the separation of two "who lived as one." In memory the two are not able to grasp (or understand) each other as before. This death has caused even "the Highest" to avert His countenance "so that nowhere may / Any deathless thing be seen against the face of Heaven or / On the green earth." Here, surely, is confirmation of the hinge-like character which Heinle's death and disappearance assumed for Benjamin. Though "hinge" may not be the most fitting word to use; "threshold," found in many of Benjamin's later writings, is perhaps better. It has a striking entrance at the beginning of the tenth of these sonnets of mourning:

> When thou dost visit me within my life
> It shall for thee but make the slightest trouble
> A step as thou didst take before to enter in my room
> Near by the threshold beckons still and even

One may leave a room to enter another by passing over a threshold, or leave one existence to enter another. Death was the threshold which allowed Benjamin to imagine his friend passing into a transcendent state and becoming available for contemplation precisely through his absence.

The deceased will never be addressed in the sonnets by name, never referred to by name. Occasionally, however, Benjamin permits himself to speak of the friend's name. This is not the name he went by on earth, but some mystical name which provides the mourner with a subject for meditation.[26] When the composer of the sonnets does address his friend directly, he resorts to "du"—whereas in life, Walter Benjamin and Fritz Heinle, whatever their intimacy, did not speak familiarly to each other.[27] That pronoun comes to function within the sonnets as the transcendental "du" used in addressing the divine.[28] Benjamin's liking for intimate obliqueness finds its outlet, too, whenever he alludes to his friend in the third person by way of a mere personal pronoun ("he," "his," or "him"). These references are numerous; often they are delayed until the last line or two of a sonnet, which intensifies their surprise effect.

Terrestrial existence is rarely on center stage in the sonnets. Mainly we are offered side views and retrospects. Several sonnets endorse Benjamin's report of a quarrel, or at least endow the friend with a nettlesome nature. So (in Sonnet 8) we hear of him as one

> Whose bitter voice chastizes me in winter
> And beneath whose gaze my tears do flow

A larger number suggest that Fritz Heinle was no ordinary human and that he left Benjamin as the martyred Christ did his followers, i.e., to ascend into Heaven. Elsewhere Heinle's conduct on earth is exalted. A few times Benjamin will break his taboo and hint at the double suicide, though without naming either party. Sonnet 28 brings images of calm—waves looming softly above the strand, westerly winds kissing cypress tips, a bride happily dreaming—to lead up to the gentle way the lovers took gas to forsake evil: "...nor dreams with more / Contented breath the well-accustomed bride

> Than did Your heads breathe out this fetid life
> Beneath blind midnight's triumph
>
> You who without anguish or delay did choose
> The way long fated . . .

For Benjamin, his friend and Rika Seligson were paragons of morality. They had refused to bargain with "blind midnight's triumph"; they had been unwilling even to inhale the same fetid air.

Here and there Benjamin manages to evoke war and battle. And yet he himself appears scarcely capable of confronting those images. It is as if he had been overmastered by another sort of reverence akin to fear and terror. The most overt war-imagery is that which concludes Sonnet 11:

> . . . a bush of gleaming bombshells
> Bent itself above his listless head
> The moon eternal wreaths his brow with beams.

More representative are glancing references to "August," the time when the war began and Heinle died, and obscurer passages which may or may not be about war. Sonnet 9 seems altogether to refer to the tribulations of war:

> Were Night to leave the inner walls
> Which linger for Your gentle stopping-place
> Then Form would detonate the sightless spell
> Greetings beckon for You from the dear departed
>
> And blooms spring open in the autumn wood
> Wherein is blazing the ensouléd fire
> Fleeing dread with each new day
> Immortality does cluster clouds about the head

For heroes sweetly scattered in their swarming
Your countenance spreads ease upon the watered green
Where winged memory finds its stride

Darkness for the careworn and their heedful ears
The melody is sinking mirrored in the blue
Yet unseals a closer land from out of morning red.

Before blind imagery like this, we would do well to suspend judgment. Especially mysterious are "Your" and "You," pointedly capitalized and in the plural. In Sonnet 28, these pronouns were seen to refer to Benjamin's dead lovers. Now the same pair may be exercising benign influence from Heaven above upon the human chaos unfolding below. But more than a few of the Heinle sonnets wish to withhold or even hide their meaning—as Benjamin was no doubt content for them to do.

A recurring feature of the poems is the similes which imply physical intimacy between the writer and his mourned friend. Thus the second quatrain of Sonnet 34:

Then came the thought: Thou sucklest me
Into thy breath I shall my self surrender
For like grapes hanging are thy lips
Which have mute witness borne to inmost things

Such images are meant to convey the intensity of the communion, no matter how problematic, which has become possible between Benjamin and his friend now that death divides them. Their rhetorical effectiveness depends on the fact that between the young men there was no physical intimacy in life.

Other passages, however, leave the impression that Benjamin did sense in himself sexual feelings for his friend — and that the friend, though aware of those feelings, did not reciprocate them. In Sonnet 35, the writer recalls how he secretly melted when his friend inquired with delicate indirection whether he (the writer) "loves his friend." Then in the very next sonnet, no. 36, comes this confession of a non-confession: "And in the friend a friendship wakes which does not guess / A quieter change of feeling in the loved one / For it blows away from open lips / That word which shelters every night with lovers." Evidently the writer of the sonnets would not then and still cannot bring himself to say: "I love you." It is hard to know how much to make of these moments, yet when Benjamin refers to "the most beautiful of men" (Sonnet 12) we had better remember the physical as well as the moral component of ideal beauty.[29]

As noted above, Benjamin addresses his departed friend as do devout persons their deity. And here one touches upon the strangest and most astonishing aspect of the sonnets: They not only imagine Fritz Heinle leaving earth and ascending to Heaven; they also impute an unearthly origin to him. Heinle was more than human, the sonnets imply, and took on human guise to visit mankind, was misunderstood and a failure — and, leaving behind disciples, returned to an invisible realm whence he had come. The idea receives its most obvious expression in Sonnet 63:

> Just as a prince will crown his undefeated way
> Into the foreign land with certain peace
> So thou with hand unstained didst of Life make
> A loyal subject ere thy taking leave
>
> Then didst thou—unacknowledged and yet shunned—
> Accept the slender palm of costly victory
> From thy faithful ones who saw thee go
> And didst no further show thyself among us

Dispersed the troop and melted into air
The land fruitless all by thee begun
Who knows how long it shall remain undone

I have made the wooing and the fearing
Of those highest days a lasting part of me
And stayed behind the writer of thy deeds.

In this scenario, Heinle only visits Life, a "foreign land"; while our sonnet writer becomes the author of a new Gospel in which the life and mission of a new Messiah is set down.

Benjamin is ready to compare his friend to Christ, but that does not mean he thinks of committing himself to Christianity. We find specifically Jewish allusions, too, and for every mention of "the Lord," there is another of "the gods." The sonnets are inclusive in their religious references. In one place Benjamin has melded German and Yiddish when referring to a Jewish ceremony of commemoration — it may be to unite with his deceased Christian friend in still another domain (see Sonnet 2). There are also a great many appearances of "the Soul." Sometimes it is the soul of the one writing; at other times it must belong to the departed. Mostly the Soul, in concert with other entities — among them Day and Night, Heaven, Death, Spirit (*Geist*), and Remembering or Memory — is called to enact fragments of allegory, and we are reminded how important that category already was for Benjamin in the years he would have been working on his sonnets.[30]

Remotely attuned, the sonnets are unlikely to shed a great deal of light on what would have been Benjamin's first response to his friend's death. For this one looks to the "Loewenson MS," a rough document drafted some weeks after the event out of concern for Wolf Heinle, the younger brother of Fritz. Its author, Erwin Loewenson, is passing on information that Wolf yearns to emulate Fritz Heinle and what he regards as his brother's Christ-like deed — yearns, that is, to protest the war by dying like his brother has.

Loewenson's (jumbled and perhaps hasty) jottings are for a letter to be sent to an unnamed party, who in turn will find someone else to intervene and so disrupt Wolf Heinle's plans. And not once but twice Loewenson mentions the influence of Walter Benjamin upon the youth. That influence is reported to be extremely harmful: Benjamin — his own words are being quoted — cannot bring himself "to accept responsibility" for disturbing the process he observes in Wolf Heinle, even if the "perfecting" of it should mean his death. Benjamin is said to be promoting a cult along with young Wolf, who sees himself reflected in Benjamin's adoration and will be half driven to follow through and kill himself because of it. Finally, we are told that Benjamin and others are so in thrall to Wolf Heinle that they have adopted his mannerisms, even his superior, above-it-all smile. Loewenson does not reveal Wolf Heinle's age: in fact he was then barely 15.[31]

The glimpse we are being given is unexpected and troubling. Here one scarcely out of childhood is being encouraged to decide whether or not to end his life, with Benjamin acting the part of a midwife who declines to intervene on either side. The drama before us suggests that Benjamin was prepared to contemplate a boy's self-annihilation as his spiritual rebirth into transcendence. More than anything, what we see through the eyes of Erwin Loewenson is a last consequence of the youth culture movement — whose aim had always been to secure for every young person the right to self-determination in the light of Spirit, or Geist. For Benjamin, these proceedings signaled the working of Spirit through a second wholly exceptional youth. We are reminded of his words commending Fritz Heinle and Rika Seligson: "You who without anguish or delay did choose / The way long fated who still happy did soon take / The path which always brought good fortune" (Sonnet 28).[32]

II. SOME TECHNICAL CONSIDERATIONS; AFTERMATH.

Outwardly, the seventy-three sonnets for Heinle maintain what is known as the Petrarchan, or "Italian," sonnet pattern. All have fourteen lines which are distributed into two quatrains followed by two tercets. Moreover, the great majority of them are cast metrically in iambic pentameter, the conventional meter for sonnets. Only a handful show metric deviations: shorter or longer lines, iambs mixed with dactyls, or a trochaic beginning. Nevertheless quite soon one senses a powerful Benjaminian countercurrent. The impulse expresses itself through long-breathed enjambments and what we may call "sprung syntax"—a deployment of syntactically connected elements over great distances, with other elements interposed. Sometimes these dispersed elements arrive in an unconventional and hence unexpected order.

Benjamin's way with enjambment and syntactic displacement, and also his elevated diction, recall Hölderlin, the late odes and hymns in particular. The stanza from *Patmos* which Benjamin took as his epigraph illustrates those tendencies exactly. In it, sprung syntax achieves the minor miracle of conveying a sundering of two minds:

> ...und wenn, ein Räthsel ewig füreinander
> Sie sich nicht fassen können
> Einander, die zusammenlebten
> Im Gedächtniß, ...

Rendered literally: "and when, a mystery eternally for one another / They cannot grasp [understand] / One another, who lived together / In memory, …" The phrase "who lived together" has interposed itself; the conventional order would have been: "and when … they who lived together cannot grasp one another in memory."

Among many similar passages in Benjamin's sonnets is one from Sonnet 24:

> Der brüderlichen Ahnung Lippen sprachen
> Nächtigt in Schluchten des Olympos Lachen
> Betenden Scherz darin das All erklinge

Rendered literally: "Lips of brotherly foreknowing spoke / Laughter spends the night in chasms of Olympos / The prayerful jest in which the universe might ring." An entire middle line interposes itself, interrupting the thrust of thought.

Appreciation for Hölderlin had begun to grow during Benjamin's youth. And Benjamin's poetry, more than any other from this time, reveals a profound engagement with him. Even Benjamin's strictness in rhyming, which verges on ruthlessness, may be traced to Hölderlin, who cast most of his mature poetry as blank verse. That is owing to the elder poet's fiercely literal approach to translating ancient Greek, demonstrated in renderings of poems by Pindar which came to light in sensational fashion in 1911, while Benjamin was still a gymnasium student.[33]

Translating Pindar, Hölderlin had striven to reproduce the grammatical and etymological features of Greek in his native language. It was often tortured in the process, but with the help of this experiment, Hölderlin was able to forge an intensely personal German idiom for his original poems.[34] All these efforts were closely examined in an essay which Benjamin considered significant, as a letter from 1917 makes apparent.[35]

Not long after, Benjamin would publish his own theory of translation; here he recommends an attitude to translation very like the one he learned from Hölderlin, through which literalness is elevated above everything else.[36]

In the sonnets, Benjamin applies a similar attitude to his treatment of end-rhymes. Rarely does he compromise a rhyming sound.[37] For the sake of a perfect end-rhyme he will terminate the line with a strikingly odd word—an archaism or a regionalism perhaps—or with a verb whose tense is wholly inconsistent. Benjamin even makes free with grammatical number. So we find Sonnet 17 beginning: "The harp hangs in the wind" and concluding: "Dost still ... discern the sound which my expiring harps / Threw out while breaking under their last grief." Especially in the original German, the discrepancy jars.

In each instance, a pure rhyme has been won at the cost of ordinary meaning, though now and then Benjamin's word order might remain blankly puzzling except for the end-rhyme, which rationalizes it. That is what happens with the final lines of Sonnet 36:

> Denn von der offnen Lippe weht sie fort
> Das nächtlich haust bei Liebenden das Wort.

Rendered literally, the last line would be: "Which nightly shelters by lovers the word." But Benjamin wants us to understand the line as "that word which nightly shelters by lovers." His rhyme justifies all.[38]

Pursuing such audacities, Benjamin—never a modest man—seeks to rival Hölderlin. Frequently, though, his poetry makes him out to be the more extreme practitioner. The sonnets for Heinle, in combining cascades of boldly displaced syntax with lines of equal length, consistent meter, and drastic rhymes, strain against themselves (almost as if they were pitting Hölderlin against himself, the original poet's swelling lines against the punitive literalism of the translator). And we are left with the question: Why would anyone deliberately draw on incompatible poetic elements when the results can only be problematic? To which our reply must be: This is the quality Benjamin sought. He was discovering a poetic analogue for his own experience of bewildering loss and transcendental gain, two things contradictory and yet forever interwoven. The burden of his poems would be expressed in their make.[39]

Readers have been forewarned that Benjamin's venture did not leave much of an echo. Still, the diary of Gershom Scholem contains important testimony: On the evening of July 1, 1918, when Scholem visited Benjamin and his then wife, Dora, he heard "some twelve" of the "fifty sonnets to Heinle," which Benjamin read out loud. Scholem found certain of them "truly remarkable." His entry continues:

> Of course, a first hearing does not allow one to say any-thing at all about them, and perhaps one's words will never find their mark as to what is most essential in them, for here is something absolutely new. I do understand most profoundly what Walter said after the reading: that this work, on which he has been laboring for three years, was and is a sufficient reason for his being utterly alone, except for me. Because in the end, he can only have a connection with persons to whom he can speak of it. I am the first to learn about all of this....He said that he had hesitated for so long to lay this before me because whole days are required for speaking of it, so that I may be provided with a basis for understanding the things which took place after his [Heinle's] death.[40]

Days before Scholem had concluded (and not for the first time) that Benjamin's life revolved about Heinle:

> But what is Walter Benjamin doing now, really? I mean: What does one see of his existence [*Dasein*], whoever can see it? Superficially: someone absolutely, fanatically, closed off from others working fanatically to justify [*begründen*] a fanatical system. Fundamentally he is entirely invisible, although he has opened himself up to me more than to all the rest who know him. In the final analysis, his whole life is nothing but a tremendous apologia for his dead friend. All that he does is intended to raise up, through methodical application, that dark center in which their friendship formed to an absolute brightness.[41]

We are left to speculate what precisely Scholem thought the "dark center" was where a friendship between Walter Benjamin and Fritz Heinle had formed. Given that Heinle is associated with darkness harboring light or hiding light in several sonnets, conceivably Scholem is merely repeating Benjamin's own words. Meanwhile there can be no mistaking the awe, tinged with discomfort, which possesses Scholem as he meditates on Benjamin's extremity of purpose.[42]

A letter from October 24, 1923, to Florens Christian Rang, Benjamin's principal correspondent for that year, makes mention of the sonnets. However, Benjamin would not attempt to publish them.[43] He had been working persistently for the publication of Heinle's poems; failure in this direction, compounded with other failures of those years, may have sufficed to discourage him, were discouragement necessary.[44] No further mentions follow; the odd, untimely works simply sank from view.[45]

36

Eventually, Heinle himself seems to have shone less bright as a figure of transcendence for Benjamin. Something the latter wrote to his confidante in June of 1934 deserves to be liberally quoted:

> What you say about his [Brecht's] influence over me causes me to recall an important and ever recurring constellation in my life. Such an influence did C. F. Heinle exert over me, in the view of my friends.... In the economy of my being, a very few relationships which could easily be counted up play a role that lets me take possession of a pole opposed to the one which is mine by nature. These relationships have always provoked more or less vehement protest in those persons closest to me.... In such a case I can do little more than entreat my friends to have faith that such ties, whose perilousness is plain to see, will show themselves to be fruitful.[46]

Here Heinle takes his place in Benjamin's personal history as part of an "ever recurring constellation." The enthralling youth had challenged Benjamin's intellectual and emotional equilibrium — but not overturned it. Even when death seemed to upend everything, Benjamin could redeem his loss with long mourning — and perhaps by atoning — in sonnets.[47]

An attempt to put these sonnets into English must reckon with their problematic character. I have chosen to dispense with end-rhyme rather than engage in the radical rewriting which would have made it possible to keep Benjamin's rhyme schemes. Moreover, my versions admit of greater variation in the length of lines, though five (iambic) feet remains the norm in them. Through such concessions, the sinews of Benjamin's syntax could be more nearly preserved — and along with them, the integrity of his thought. Nevertheless, English lacks certain syntactic resources available to German — resources which Benjamin exploits so effectively for his stylistic daring. It is also true that native German speakers tend to recoil from the quixotic aspect of Benjamin's originals, and some go so far as to prefer the compromised English versions offered by me.

A final thought: Walter Benjamin would have deplored any translation of his sonnets. To imagine them in the hands of a close friend was already too much. In later years Gershom Scholem, who believed that Benjamin's sonnets had vanished with his death, was wistful:

> I was always wanting to make a copy of them,
> but unfortunately I could never move Walter to
> agree to it. Other writings which I copied during
> the first years of our friendship...were kept safe
> in my possession.[48]

ESSAY NOTES

1.   The manuscripts containing Benjamin's Heinle sonnets were deposited by Bataille in the Bibliothèque nationale, Paris, where they were recovered by Giorgio Agamben in 1981, that is, some forty-one years later. The German edition of Benjamin's sonnets by Suhrkamp Verlag appeared in 1986 (under the title *Sonette*, edited and with an afterword by Rolf Tiedemann).

2.   Benjamin's essay *"Über das Programm der kommenden Philosophie"* [On the Programme of the Coming Philosophy], written in 1918, contains his prospectus for renewing German philosophy along Kantian lines. A letter to Gershom Scholem dated 20 January 1930 gives clear expression to Benjamin's second ambition: "I have already carved out a reputation for myself, although of modest proportions. The goal I had set for myself has not yet been fully realized, but I am finally nearing it. That goal is to be considered the foremost critic of German literature."

3.   Arendt's essay on Benjamin, which did so much to excite the interest of the English-speaking world, was first issued as a magazine article in *The New Yorker* (19 October 1968) under the title "Reflections. Walter Benjamin." That same year the article was reprinted to serve as the introduction for *Illuminations*, her collection of writings by Benjamin, the first to appear in English.

4.   As per entries in Scholem's diary for June 25 and July 1, 1918. Scholem, born in Berlin in 1897 as Gerhard Scholem, emigrated to Palestine in 1923 and there won an international reputation for his scholarly studies of Judaism and the Kabbalah. He remains the best as well as the only abundant source for Benjamin's attitudes on matters personal and intellectual, especially for the years 1915 through 1923.

5.   See, among others, the afterword by Rolf Tiedemann to the original German edition of the sonnets (Suhrkamp Verlag, 1986); the entry "Die Sonette an Heinle" by Reinhold Görling for Benjamin Handbuch: *Leben — Werk — Wirkung*; and *Walter Benjamin: A Critical Life*, by Howard Eiland and Michael W. Jennings (Belknap Press of Harvard University, 2014). The last-named says this: "Benjamin's relationship with Heinle — which would last for little more than a year — is one of the most enigmatic episodes in Benjamin's enigmatic life. At once epochal and impenetrable, the encounter with Heinle would leave a deep mark on Benjamin's intellectual and emotional physiognomy for years to come" (p. 53). Yet there is almost no informed comment provided for the sonnets themselves.

6.   Benjamin was far from the only one to cultivate the sonnet in early 20th-century Germany. Especially influential would have been Stefan George, whose translation ("Umdichtung") of Shakespeare's complete sonnets appeared in 1909. Many of the expressionist poets also produced examples. Rilke's *Die Sonette an Orpheus*, fifty-five in number, were written in 1922 and appeared in the following year while Benjamin may still have been at work on his own sonnets. Intellectually fine sonnets by Goethe and the many accomplished sonnets written by German Romantic poets, e.g., August Wilhelm Schlegel and August von Platen, were also sure to have interested him.

7.   No letters from Benjamin to Heinle or from Heinle to Benjamin are known. It is the general case that comparatively few letters addressed to Benjamin survive, whereas many who received Benjamin's letters took the trouble to preserve his.

8.   Walter Benjamin (15 VII 1892—27 IX 1940) was born to affluent parents and grew to manhood in the western quarters of Berlin, in an assimilated Jewish milieu. His childhood and adolescence are recounted in two autobiographical texts; besides the *Berliner Chronik*, which Benjamin left as a fragment, there is *Berliner Kindheit um 1900* [Berlin Childhood ca. 1900], which soon followed and in which the remembering subject is kept anonymous and distanced from the author. Christopf Friedrich Heinle (1 III 1894—8 VIII 1914) was born at Mayen in der Eifel, where his Protestant father held a modest position in the civil service as a "königliche Regierungsassessor"; his mother was Roman Catholic. He attended gymnasium in Aachen and then university in Göttingen before meeting up with Walter Benjamin. What we know of him and his poetry today is owing to his friendship with Benjamin.

40

9.   More than forty lyrics by Heinle survive. These are reproduced in the dissertation of Dr. Johannes Steizinger: *Revolte, Eros und Sprache. Walter Benjamins 'Metaphysik der Jugend'* [Revolt, eros, and language. Walter Benjamin's "Metaphysik der Jugend"]. PhD diss., U. Wien, 2012.

10.   Benjamin would maintain a complicated view of his own relationship to things German and to Germany. A lengthy and thoughtful letter to his gentile friend Rang (22 November 1923) asserts his awareness of being deeply bound to German culture but also expresses his conviction that, in times of crisis such as they were then living through, it was not fitting for a Jew to take public positions on matters critical to the nation. "In a people's most terrible moments," writes Benjamin, "only those belonging to that people are called to speak, or even more, only those belonging in the most eminent sense, those who can say not only *mea res agitur* [my interest is involved] but *propriam rem ago* [I am acting here in my own affair]. It is not for a Jew to speak."
    When young Benjamin, writing to Herbert Blumenthal, a fellow Jew, remarks on the Germanness of his new friend Heinle, he already implies that Heinle is more German than they are.

11.   The original text of Heinle's poem, as per Benjamin: "Aus gelben Linnen steigt gebräunt und klar / Der schmale Hals grad. Aber sehr bewußt / Verschenkter Feste sinkt versengtes Paar / In schönen Bogen zu geschweifter Lust. / Wie dunkle Trauben springt der Lippen Paar / Vor jäher Reife zu bewegter Brust." Incidentally, there is much in Benjamin's early letters on relations between the sexes, which were felt to be in urgent need of reform by the progressive young.

12.   The "youth culture movement" made up a tiny sliver of the prewar German youth phenomenon. Nevertheless, the group's challenge to authority brought about routine police surveillance of its meetings, and debates were even held in the legislatures of Bavaria and Prussia during which conservatives urged suppression of *Der Anfang*, a publication with no more than 800 paid subscribers; Siegfried Bernfeld, the group leader in Vienna, would claim later that only 3,000 young people had been active in the Jugendkulturbewegung across Germany and Austria. (It was remarked by hostile observers that most of them appeared to be Jews.)

Student contributors to *Der Anfang* expressed themselves freely but only under various pseudonyms, out of fear of reprisal; Benjamin's pieces appeared under the name "Ardor." Freedom of expression was also promoted in so-called "speech forums," or *Sprechsäle*, which university students organized for students of high-school age, to give them the chance to discuss issues of importance to themselves without adult supervision. And as a matter of course both Benjamin and Heinle belonged to the progressive Berlin chapter of the Freie Studentenschaft, a national federation of students unaffiliated with the traditional dueling fraternities and welcoming to Jews, Roman Catholics, women, and those of modest means. (Members of the traditional fraternities were held to be "bound" in honor to their organizations; hence anyone who did not so belong could be regarded as a "free" student.) The fundamental goals of the Freie Studentenschaft were to liberalize German schools and universities and to better the status of "free" students. At the end of the winter semester 1913–14 Benjamin assumed the leadership of the Berlin chapter of the Freie Studentenschaft, a position to which he was reelected. These political involvements are described most fully in the *Berlin Chronicle* (notices 12 and 13).

13. Letter to Carla Seligson (17 November 1913). Beneath their political disagreements ran deeper currents of dissension: "Once more [continues Benjamin] I understood the *inevitability of the idea* which pits me against Heinle. I wish for that fulfillment which one can but wait for, and he [i.e., God] fulfill. But the fulfillment is something which is too much at rest and too divine to issue from something other than the burning wind. Yesterday I said to Heinle: 'Each of us is religious, but it is a matter of how one believes in his belief.'"

14. Momme Brodersen's *Klassenbild mit Walter Benjamin* (2012) informs us that of the 22 members in Benjamin's class which graduated from the Kaiser-Friedrich-Schule, Charlottenburg (Berlin), in the year 1912, five perished on the battlefields of World War I. Five others were seriously wounded one or more times. In answering the call to arms, the graduates were following their teachers, many of whom were reserve officers in Prussian regiments. The only member in this class to escape military service was Walter Benjamin himself. The histories of its thirteen Jewish members are of particular interest: Alfred Steinfeld died from accidental mercury poisoning during his military training for the ambulance corps; seven other Jewish graduates would receive the Iron Cross, first and/or second class, for

wartime service; Benjamin and three more ended up dying directly or indirectly from Nazi persecution, the earliest already in 1937.

15. See *Berlin Chronicle*, notice 12. Heinle's lover, Friederike ("Rika") Seligson (1891-1914), had two younger sisters, Charlotte ("Carla," 1892-1965) and Gertrud ("Traute," 1895-1915; she would also commit suicide with a lover). In his Berlin memoir Benjamin refers to "those three sisters about whom everything in those days always gravitated" and adds: "—as if a Jewish widow living together with her three daughters should represent the right sort of fulcrum for a group [i.e., of radical students] bent on the annihilation of the family unit." The Seligsons lived just west of the Tiergarten at Schleswiger Ufer 15; the "Heim," a simple rented space, was close by at Brücken-Allee 9. Heinle's apartment found itself in this neighborhood, too. Benjamin at the time lived with his parents in an imposing new house in Grunewald, a wealthy district on the western outskirts of Berlin.

Several Berlin papers carried brief reports of the double suicide, even though in these first August days local news was being crowded out in favor of war-related items. Thus the evening edition of the *Berliner Tageblatt* for Monday, August 10, 1914, beneath the heading "Suicide and Unhappiness in Love": "In a room of the Amt für Soziale Arbeit of the Berliner Freie Studentenschaft, the 20-year-old university student Friedrich Heinle has poisoned himself by inhaling gas, along with his 23-year-old girlfriend, Erika Seligson, who lived with her mother near the Schleswiger Tor. When the deed was discovered, death had already claimed them both. A note left behind indicates that the pair sought death being unhappy in love."

Selbſtmord aus Liebeskummer. In einem Raum des Amtes für ſoziale Arbeit der Berliner Freien Studentenſchaft vergiftete ſich geſtern der zwanzigjährige, aus Maßen ſtammende Student Friedrich Heinle mit ſeiner 23 Jahre alten Braut Erika Seligſon, die bei ihrer Mutter am Schleswiger Tor wohnte, durch Einatmen von Leuchtgas. Als man die Tat bemerkte, war bei beiden Perſonen der Tod ſchon eingetreten. Aus einem hinterlaſſenen Schreiben geht hervor, daß beide aus Liebeskummer den Tod geſucht haben. —

The suicides of C. Friedrich "Fritz" Heinle and
Friederike "Rika" Seligson as reported in the Berliner Tageblatt for
Monday, August 10, 1914 (evening edition).

16. *Berlin Chronicle* (notice 13). Berlin cafés were gathering places for young radicals who opposed the official culture of Wilhelmine Germany. Benjamin and Heinle transacted much of their political business at night in their favorite cafés. Notice 13 of the *Chronicle* is filled with Benjamin's affectionate recollections of them.

17. In fact, he never took up his second term. Benjamin also broke dramatically with his mentor, Gustav Wyneken, the adult leader of the progressive youth movement, after he endorsed the cause of the war in a speech given in November 1914 before Munich students and titled "Der Krieg und die Jugend" [The War and Youth]. Benjamin's rebuke of Wyneken (9 March 1915) begins: "Dear Herr Dokter Wyneken, I ask that you accept the following lines, wherewith I absolutely and unreservedly renounce you, as the final proof of my loyalty, and of that only."

18. Even before, Benjamin's letters rarely alluded to public events. Those written during July of 1914, when the diplomatic crisis which led to war was brewing, make no mention of them; they continue to be taken up with student politics, literary matters, and personal affairs. Nor do those coming after Heinle's suicide often refer to his death or to the fighting. In *Walter Benjamin: The Story of a Friendship*, Scholem claims that Benjamin was so averse to discussing the war that he would have little to do with anyone who neglected his wishes in this regard. Towards the beginning of their own acquaintance, on the other hand, Benjamin had asked Scholem to search out hard-to-come-by information bearing on the question of how much Germany and Austria might be to blame for the conflict (*Friendship*, pp. 23-24).

19. Letter to Siegfried Bernfeld (11 October 1914). To be sure, Benjamin was not always able to shun discussion of the ongoing war when writing to his close friends. A letter to Herbert Blumenthal (Belmore) from late in the year 1916 dismisses the practice of "objective criticism" before such an engulfing catastrophe:

> I have learned that in the Night, bridges and flights do
> not help, only brotherly striding through it. And we are
> in the middle of the Night. Once I sought to combat
> it with words (Thomas Mann had published his vul-
> gar *Gedanken im Kriege*). At that time I learned that
> whoever struggles against the Night must stir its deepest

darkness so that it puts forth its light, and that in this
tremendous life-effort, words are but one station: and
can be the end-station only where they are never the first
station. . . . It is all too big to criticize. It is all the Night
bearing Light, the bleeding body of Spirit [*des Geistes*].

20.   *Youth* is the pivotal term in an entry in Gershom Scholem's diary for November 25, 1917. The entry concerns Benjamin's essay "Der Idiot *von Dostoevski*" [*The Idiot* by Dostoevsky], written earlier that year. Scholem is speculating on how Benjamin had felt Fritz Heinle's death: "For the theory [that Prince Myshkin is not a character subject to empirical psychology but the expression of "an immortal life"] seems to have been passed on to him [Benjamin] by a teacher, namely, by his dead friend. He saw in him the essence of youth; and through him he saw, too, how youth dies. Inconceivable, extraordinary, how Walter Benjamin could survive the death of his friend. That he succeeded in giving up his own youth — this the first wonder — and yet went on living with the *idea* of it leaves me speechless." (See also note 23, below.)

21.   There is one bit of external evidence to help with the dating: In the summer of 1918, Benjamin confided to Gershom Scholem that he had been working for three years on the sonnets for Heinle. By then Benjamin had already made up a set of fifty of them (Scholem, *Tagebücher*, II, p. 263; see also notes 40 and 41).
      The Heinle sonnets are preserved in several manuscript collections at the Walter Benjamin Archiv in Berlin. WBA 253 contains fifty items, presumably the same as those which Benjamin showed to Scholem, and which he must have planned to publish as a set; the nine sonnets of WBA 254 display somewhat more variability in meter and line length as well as manner; WBA 255 holds fourteen more. Other, related material having to do with the sonnets is found in WBA 256. The sonnets are presented as individual fair copies, some bearing revisions which are for the most part minor. The variation in Benjamin's handwriting and in inks and paper types suggest that these copies could have been made over a period of as much as ten years. In certain cases, themes or images employed in the second and third groups of sonnets are also used in sonnets belonging to the set of fifty; it is possible that, for Benjamin, items in the main set replaced similar items from the other groups (see also notes 37, 39, and 40).

22. The first version is titled *Dichtermuth* [Poet's Courage]; the second, *Blödigkeit* [Timidity]. Benjamin characterizes them as the first and final stages of a complex process of writing and rewriting, but actually *Dichtermuth* comes late in the series of which *Blödigkeit*, 1803, is indeed the last. This essay remained unpublished during Benjamin's lifetime.

23. The MS of the essay does not bear any dedication. Benjamin's remarks appeared in *Die literarische Welt* for July 13, 1928, under the rubric "Über Stefan George," along with anniversary reflections which had been solicited from sundry others as well.

 That Benjamin viewed Fritz Heinle as "a figure akin to Hölderlin" is confirmed by Gershom Scholem (*Friendship*, p. 17). In the same place Scholem remarks that "death had moved his friend [Heinle] to the realm of the sacrosanct." But Benjamin was discovering Heinle everywhere: After Scholem informed him that he could see the figure of Fritz Heinle behind Benjamin's understanding of Dostoevsky's Prince Myshkin (note 20, above), Benjamin, deeply touched, replied by express letter (3 December 1917):

> I often feel in a celebratory mood since receiving your
> letter. It is as though I have entered a holiday
> period, and I am obliged to revere as Revelation
> that which has revealed itself to you.

In the sonnets, Benjamin frequently likens Heinle to Christ himself.

24. By striking such attitudes Benjamin aligns himself with a venerable tradition. The elegies of Catullus already furnish examples as memorable as any of the poet who becomes the suffering subject in his poems about love; the European sonnet, too, may be said to live from this convention.

25. Between 1914 and 1922, that is, during the same years he was writing the sonnets for Heinle, Benjamin carried out another significant poetry-related project: translating a portion of Baudelaire's *Les fleurs du mal* (the "Tableaux parisiens" poems, for which he maintained both meter and rhyme schemes; published in 1923; see note 36). He also translated other poems by Baudelaire.

 In general, this was the period in Benjamin's life when he showed the most interest in poetry. His early letters bespeak a lively attention to what was being produced by near contemporaries, Rilke and George among them. He enjoyed taking part in poetry readings and "had a beautiful voice, melodious and easily remembered" (Scholem, *Friendship*, p. 8; see also pp. 64-66). With Heinle he wrote a set of humorous verses titled *Urwaldgeister* [Spirits of the Primal Wood].

In the early 1920s, towards the end of this period, Benjamin wrote at least six more sonnets, one to his wife and five to Jula Cohn (a seventh, written for another inamorata, dates from 1933; see Appendix II for texts and translations). Moreover, late in 1932, while his mind was grappling with memories of childhood, Benjamin drafted a substantial amount of verse which he then recast for *Berlin Childhood ca. 1900* — a work whose subtly cadenced prose recalls poetry.

26. Medieval kabbalism was an important influence; see the commentary for Sonnet 1 and also for nos. 61 and 71.

27. Evidence for a formal mode of address between the two lies in Benjamin's report of Heinle's words to him in the latter's message announcing the double suicide: "Sie werden uns im Heim liegen finden." The letter from Benjamin to Carla Seligson also quotes Heinle addressing him formally: "Ich hätte Ihnen wohl eigentlich sehr vieles zu sagen." It was customary for adherents of the Jugendkulturbewegung to address one another with "Sie" and not "du," and at the same time to refer to one another as comrades. (The Wandervögel used "du" as well as "comrade" with one another.)

28. The translator of these sonnets has allowed Benjamin the sonnet writer to address his deceased friend with *thou* (*thine*, *thee*) in place of the usual *you* (*yours*, *you*). The former, a venerable second-person singular pronoun, finds use today almost solely in religious or spiritual contexts, for calling on the divine. (No such distinction exists in German between a familiar second-person singular and a special second-person singular reserved for religious purposes: Martin Buber's famous book from 1923, known in English as *I and Thou*, goes by the title *Ich und Du* in the original German.)

The everyday plural pronoun *you* (capitalized as *You* to match Benjamin's orthography) comes into play in the present translations whenever Benjamin addresses his friend Heinle and Rika Seligson together.

29. Benjamin's shy admissions of love for his deceased friend contrast with the lascivious hints of relations between the spiritual leader and his male disciples that season many poems in Stefan George's collection *Stern des Bundes* (1914).

30. Moreover, the poems for Heinle are fertile incubators of ideas and "thought-figures" (*Denkfiguren*) known to us from Benjamin's later writings. It is worth observing that in the context of the sonnets, one cannot really distinguish what is religious from what is philosophical. During the time he was writing them, Benjamin held the idea of God to be indispensable to truth and to transcendental experience—in his view, the only sort of experience which finally mattered. For example, an appeal to God as the ultimate philosophical underpinning is found in Benjamin's essay *Über das Programm der kommenden Philosophie* (1918). But there is a similar appeal, to "theology," in the first of the fifteen theses which make up Benjamin's late work *Über den Begriff der Geschichte* [Concerning the Concept of History] (1940).

31. Johann Wolfgang Heinle was born in Arnsberg (Westphalia) on June 26, 1899. As for the date of the Lowenson MS, it cannot have been produced in the immediate wake of Fritz Heinle's suicide; still, it must stem from a time not long after: The writer is proposing that a friend send condolences to Wolf Heinle and say that he has just learned of the suicides of Fritz Heinle and Rika Seligson. Somewhere between late August and late September 1914 would seem a sensible guess.

32. Wolf Heinle did not, in the end, commit suicide (see note 47). Whether or not a letter was ever sent on his behalf, and if so to whom, is unclear. Erwin Loewenson (1888–1963) was active in the expressionist circles of prewar Berlin, a leading member of the theater group Der Neue Club and, along with Benjamin, a contributor to *Der Anfang*. See Appendix I for an English translation of the Loewenson MS drawing on a transcription provided in Steizinger (*Revolte, Eros und Sprache*).

The place of suicide in Benjamin's youthful milieu is too large a topic to be broached, except to observe that it was often resorted to. (As an influence one would point to the expressionist movement, then at fever pitch, and to its glamorization of decisive action.) Benjamin himself in after years would suffer from depressions which he imagined only death could relieve; the most serious culminated in the weeks and months before his fortieth birthday, in 1932, when he made elaborate plans for carrying out suicide. Fleeing Vichy France in September 1940, he brought along a quantity of morphine and so was able to kill himself when Spanish authorities seemed about to send him back. At the time of his sonnets, Benjamin was taken up with the suicidal aspirations of others but already sensed a similar impulse in himself (see Sonnet 25 and the commentary for it; see also the sonnet "In trüben Gedanken," Appendix II, no. 2, and commentary).

33. Renewed interest in Hölderlin, and in his later poetry especially, was hastened by the discovery, in 1909, of manuscripts containing translations that Hölderlin had made of Pindar's major poems. Norbert von Hellingrath, the young scholar responsible for the discovery, caused it to become widely known two years later when he published his essay *Pindarübertragungen von Hölderlin: Prolegomena zu einer Erstausgabe* [Pindar Translations by Hölderlin: Prolegomena to a First Edition]. In 1913 von Hellingrath issued the first two volumes of an edition of Hölderlin's poetry and other writings. Pindar's verse in the language of Hölderlin would receive ardent furthering through Stefan George.

Rilke, too, was beginning to be influenced by Hölderlin in these years. Not so long before he sat down to write the first of his "Duino" elegies, in 1912, he was shown drafts of some Hölderlin hymns by von Hellingrath.

34. For more on Hölderlin's Pindar translations, see David Constantine, "Hölderlin's Pindar: The Language of Translation," *The Modern Language Review* 73/4 (October 1978), pp. 825–34.

35. The letter, addressed to Ernst Schoen (27 February 1917), contains one of Benjamin's rare comments bearing on the war:

> Have you read that Norbert von Hellingrath is fallen? I had wanted to give him my Hölderlin study to read when he returned. The thematic standpoint he adopted in his work on [Hölderlin's] Pindar translation was the outward spur for my study. Incidentally, he intended to write a comprehensive book on Hölderlin.

Von Hellingrath had died on December 1, 1916, during the battle of Verdun. The edition of Hölderlin's works which he began would be completed by others and run to six volumes.

Von Hellingrath's essay *Pindarübertragungen von Hölderlin* appeals to ancient literary theory so as to establish a distinction in poetic practice between "smooth" and "rough [hard] facture [*Fügung*]." In the first of these, music and atmosphere conspire to overcome discreteness and the plain, immediate sense of words; one expects to encounter innumerable conventional verbal flourishes and stereotyped images whose purpose is to engender a lulling euphony. In the second, the individual words and phrases assert themselves, each against the rest; the poetic formations are less rational, less easily scanned. With rough facture no more than the individual word tends to coincide with the metrical unit; with smooth facture, though, an image or some other larger element is coordinated with the meter more often than not.

Smooth facture usually employs lines of even length; favors end-rhyme; and causes the ideas which are expressed to begin and end with the lines. Enjambments will remain exceptional. Rough facture delights in defined, complicated thoughts which overspill the ends of lines, sometimes several or even more; and favors blank verse and flexible line length over regular lines and constraining rhyme-schemes. In place of the conventional diction to which the former is hospitable, the latter prefers plain words or else odd or strange ones — anything, that is, but routine poetic language. Finally, smooth facture suits short lyric verse whereas rough facture readily sustains greater poetic spans (this last point is merely implied).

Having drawn a broad distinction between types of poetic facture, von Hellingrath sets up Hölderlin as the great modern German master of rough facture and moves on to offer a nuanced comparison of numerous Pindar translations into German. His essay points up Hölderlin's insistence on a literal translation of Pindar as well as the relationship of that literalism to rough facture.

36. Issued as the preface for his translation of Baudelaire's "Tableaux parisiens" poems from *Les fleurs du mal* (see note 25). The preface (written in 1921) is titled "Die Aufgabe des Übersetzers" [The Duty of the Translator]. "No poem is intended for the reader," says Benjamin at the outset. That is, poems exist for themselves; translations have a greater duty to the original text than to any reader. Merely to convey the manifest content of the original in translation is a trivial accomplishment. In fact, a good translation will remain problematic, being haunted by an original which refuses to be dissolved in the second language. In practice, translators should import the formal features of the language of the original text into whatever language the text is translated into, so that a kind of palimpsest results.

Benjamin considered it his duty to produce truthful metrical versions of Baudelaire's poems, in order to let their eccentric diction ("the Baroque of banality") come into focus. After spending up to nine years translating the poems and reworking his translations, he would conclude that he had failed (on seeing his work in print; letters to Florens Christian Rang and Hugo von Hofmannsthal, January 1924).

37. Fewer than a dozen instances of approximate end-rhyme are found in the seventy-three sonnets; and only one of these (in Sonnet 27) is egregious (*Geliebten / getrübten*).

As concerns their rhyme, Benjamin's sonnets are not Petrarchan. The principal rhyme patterns in Petrarch's sonnets (of which there are 317 in his collection of lyric poetry known as the *Canzoniere* [Songbook]) are *abba abba cde cde* and *abba abba cdc dcd*. Benjamin's preferred scheme, on the other hand, is *abba baab cdc dee*, found in fully thirty of the fifty sonnets in his main grouping. It is interesting that the second group in Benjamin's MS collection of sonnets (nos. 51–59) does not show a single example of the rhyme scheme which dominates the first group, while the third group (nos. 60–73) resembles the first in its schemes. Altogether, fifty of his sonnets employ the *abba baab* pattern in their quatrains and nineteen *abba abba*, while the remaining four make use of *abab cdcd* (Sonnet 1), *aabb aabb* (no. 41), *abab baba* (no. 58), and *abab abab* (no. 60); and there are nineteen different tercet patterns. Such flexible handling of the tercets is combined with reliance on the terminal rhyming couplet, employed in no less than fifty-three of the Heinle sonnets. This device, absent from Petrarch's sonnets, is important inasmuch as it makes possible a dramatic twist to the argument at the last moment. (Benjamin would have come to appreciate its effectiveness from reading Shakespeare's sonnets in the translations by Stefan George.) Benjamin respects the Petrarchan limit of five end-rhymes to a sonnet (he may employ as few as two). By way of exception, the standard Shakespearean scheme calling for seven rhymes — which Shakespeare distributes over three quatrains and a concluding rhyming couplet — namely, as *abab cdcd efef gg* — is reserved for the sonnet which Benjamin placed first in his main set of fifty.

38. During the years 1914–24 Benjamin was extremely unorthodox in matters of punctuation, and in his personal letters made almost no use at all of commas (Scholem, *Walter Benjamin Briefe*, I, p. 11). Each of his Heinle sonnets ends with a period (or question mark), but aside from these only some dozen-and-a-half instances of punctuation — dashes single and paired, colons, question marks, or quotation marks — are found in the whole run. No periods appear before the conclusion of any sonnet (all of them contain at least two grammatically independent thoughts) and commas are entirely absent. There are many places in the sonnets where commas or some other element of punctuation would make Benjamin's meaning clearer. However, in the case of the line "Das nächtlich haust bei Lieb-

enden das Wort," punctuation (before "das Wort") would only encourage misreading. The present translator has respected Benjamin's minimalist punctuating nearly to the letter.

39. Quite apart from Hölderlin (or von Hellingrath), Benjamin had read Greek and Latin masters both "smooth" and "rough" while a schoolboy. Shakespeare and Donne suggest themselves as yet another source of technical inspiration, but Benjamin, little acquainted with English, would not have known their poetry firsthand.

One may hypothesize that "rough facture" was not always on Benjamin's mind. It could be that those sonnets which affect a polished Hellenism — nos. 51 and 73 being striking examples — antedate his exploration of Hölderlinian roughness, which in any case adheres far less to the middle group of sonnets (nos. 51–59). Conversely, none of the sonnets in the main group (nos. 1–50) are sleekly pagan. A diplomatic edition of the Heinle sonnets being prepared under the auspices of the Walter Benjamin Archiv, Berlin, should shed light on the relative chronology of the three groups of sonnets as Benjamin left them.

40. Scholem, *Tagebücher*, II, p. 263. Benjamin and his wife, the daughter of Leon Kellner, a Viennese English professor and Shakespeare specialist (and prominent Zionist), were living in Bern. They had married on April 17, 1917, and their only child, Stefan Rafael, was weeks old (having been born on April 11, 1918). The Benjamins' marriage was already deteriorating, to go by ear- and eye-witness accounts left by Scholem.

Earlier the same diary passage was cited as evidence for the dating of Benjamin's sonnets (see note 21). Benjamin also contemplated issuing his poems in sets of less than fifty, as can be seen from WBA 256, which preserves (among other things) two schemes for sets of thirty. Common to these schemes are the following twenty-five sonnets from WBA 253: nos. 1, 2, 5, 14, 15, 20–29, 33-37, 41, 44–46, and 50. Each scheme lists five additional sonnets from WBA 253 which are not included in the other one. Supplementary or alternative items designated with letters of the alphabet and presumably coming from WBA 254 and/or 255 are listed after the numbered items in each scheme.

41. Ibid., p. 256. Dated 25 June 1918.

42.   Scholem would have been uneasy with Benjamin's glorification of Fritz Hein-le's act. His suicide was not to be squared with religion, whether Jewish or Chris-tian, and so long as Benjamin was entirely bent on justifying it, Scholem could describe him as striving "fanatically" to "justify a fanatical system."

But then Scholem — who yearned to see more Jewishness in his cherished friend — would have appreciated that the sonnets for Heinle do comply in other ways with Judaism. Most telling in this regard is how scrupulously they realize traditional sonnet form. If traditional Judaism observes ancient rules even as it accommodates modern life, a similar strategy operates in the sonnets — where the literalism Benjamin took from Hölderlin as translator is made to confront free-doms he borrowed from Hölderlin the original poet. Again, one thinks of Benja-min's frequently expressed suspicion of "images," that is, of the specific memories he retains of his departed friend, and of his refusal to address the friend by name, a form of deference reserved traditionally for God. And with respect to another fundamental Jewish value, that of atonement, Benjamin's severe enactment of son-net form can be understood as a chastisement of himself in keeping with its ritual demands. So viewed, the entire sonnets project begins to look like Walter Benja-min's atonement, performed over many years, for falling short of his friend. Cer-tainly his sonnets obey the Jewish imperative to remember (that is, never to forget) the dead.

Scholem's memoir of his own friendship with Benjamin, written more than three decades after Benjamin's death, contains no searching reflections upon the sonnets. There he professes himself unable to explain why Benjamin had valued Heinle's poetry so, and speaks of a "mystery" (*Friendship*, p. 66).

43.   Benjamin had besought Rang to intervene with Hugo von Hofmannsthal, editor of the prestigious literary journal *Neue deutsche Beiträge*, with the aim of promoting the work of Fritz Heinle and Wolf Heinle along with his own. "I should think," he wrote to Rang, "that six weeks would be enough for him [von Hofmannsthal] to receive an impression at leisure.... I thought it best to refrain for now from sending him samples of my sonnets." Ultimately von Hofmannsthal would publish Benjamin's Goethe essay in his journal, in two installments, but he would not be sufficiently impressed with Heinle's poems to accept any.

44.   A letter dated 20 December 1922, once again addressed to Rang, mentions the talk on Heinle and his lyric poetry which Benjamin had given in Heidelberg

at the home of Marianne Weber, widow of the eminent sociologist and political economist Max Weber. This talk, which drew on Benjamin's introduction for his prospective edition of the works of Heinle, met with incomprehension (see the *Berlin Chronicle*, notice 12, for another account). In a slightly earlier letter to Rang (14 October) Benjamin had reported that he was continuing work on the introduction but warned that he could no longer count on publication. Benjamin had also hoped to feature Heinle's poetry in a journal of his own, to be called *Angelus novus*; but the undertaking failed to receive financial backing and never materialized. A trove of Heinle poems of which Benjamin was the jealous possessor for many years disappeared in the wake of his hurried departure from Germany in 1933.

45.   Except for the appearance of two lines from one of the sonnets as an epigraph in Benjamin's collection of short writings and aphorisms published under the title *Einbahnsstraße* [One-way Street; 1928]; see the commentary for Sonnet 42.

46.   Letter to Gretel Karplus (later the wife of Theodor Wiesengrund Adorno), early June 1934. Benjamin's more intimate epistolary confessions were offered to women friends such as Carla Seligson and Gretel Karplus (Adorno).

47.   In a letter to Rang dated 24 February 1923, Benjamin rendered his definitive tribute to Fritz Heinle and to his brother Wolf, the latter having died some three weeks before (of natural causes):

> And on top of that, death: The dying of the few persons through whom one had the standard for one's own life, despite the incommensurability. Recently I read in Poe — the passage is not to hand — in the beginning of a novella — something approximately like this: that there is a kind of thinking which is not sophism, a creating which is not copying, a conduct that is without calculation — some few values which caused me suddenly to remember with blinding intensity that these persons — who are being fused in memory but who were very distinct for me as long as they, as long one of them lived, who seemed truly

to come from another world in their youth, which they did not survive — *had* lived. And thus, just as there may be an unmistakable and classic expression of beauty in women, so of these two youths I sometimes say to myself that no one in whom there resides a knowledge of the noble life would ever have failed to recognize immediately that it [the noble life] existed in them.

48.   Letter to Ernst Schoen, 28 November 1960 (Scholem, *Briefe*, II, p. 73). Scholem could not have known (then) that Benjamin himself had taken pains to insure the survival of his sonnets.

SONNETS

Wenn aber stirbt alsdenn
An dem am meisten
Die Schönheit hieng, daß an der Gestalt
Ein Wunder war and die Himmlischen gedeutet
Auf ihn, und wenn, ein Räthsel ewig füreinander
Sie sich nicht fassen können
Einander, die zusammenlebten
Im Gedächtniß, und nicht den Sand nur oder
Die Weiden es hinwegnimmt und die Tempel
Ergreift, wenn die Ehre
Des Halbgotts und der Seinen
Verweht und selber sein Angesicht
Der Höchste wendet
Darob, daß nirgend ein
Unsterbliches mehr am Himmel zu sehn ist oder
auf grüner Erde, was ist

When now he comes to die
Upon whom beauty did most
Hang, so that in his form
A wonder was and the Heaven-powers pointed
At him, and when, a lasting mystery each for the other
They cannot each other grasp
Who lived as one in memory
And not the sand only or
The willows it removes and seized are
The temples, when the honor of
The half-god passes and that of his followers
And even His countenance
The Highest turns
Away so that nowhere may
Any deathless thing be seen against the face of Heaven or
On the green earth — What is this?

from *Patmos*, Friedrich Hölderlin

01

Enthebe mich der Zeit der du entschwunden
Und löse mir von innen deine Nähe
Wie rote Rosen in den Dämmerstunden
Sich lösen aus der Dinge lauer Ehe

Wahrhaftge Huldigkeit und bittre Stimme
Entbehr ich heiter und der Lippen Röte
Die überbrannt war von der schwarzen Glimme
Des Haares purpurn schattend Stirn der Nöte

Und auch das Abbild mag sich mir versagen
Von Zorn und Loben wie du sie mir botest
Des Gangs in dem du herzoglich getragen

Die Fahne deren Sinnbild du erlotest
Wenn nur in mir du deinen heilgen Namen
Bildlos errichtest wie unendlich Amen.

Disburden me of Time from which thou'rt vanished
And of thy presence free me from within
As in the twilight hours red roses free themselves
From all mere marriedness of things

The heartfelt homage and the bitter voice
I forego calmly and thy burning lips
And yet more burning brow enshaded purple
Just below the black gleam of thy hair

So may that image fail me too of praise
And ire which thou wouldst offer
Underway while very like a prince

Thou didst the banner bear its symbol to unriddle
Plant in me thy sacred Name instead
Name without image Amen without end.

02

Hättest du der Welt dein Sterben prophezeit
Natur wär dir vorangeeilt im Tode
Kehrte mit unerbittlichem Gebote
Das Sein in ewige Vergessenheit

Am Himmel ständen sanfte Morgenrote
Zur Stunde da hinglitt dein Körperkleid
Die Wälder färbte alle schwarzes Leid
Nacht überzog das Meer auf leisem Boote

Aus Sternen bildet namenlose Trauer
Das Denkmal deines Blicks am Himmelsbogen
Und Finsternis verwehrt mit dichter Mauer

Des neuen Frühlings Licht heraufgezogen
Die Jahrzeit sieht im stillen Stand der Sterne
Aus deines Todes spiegelnder Zisterne.

Hadst thou foretold thy dying to the world
Nature were before thee gone in death
And by implacable decree would
Being turn to blankness without end

Tender morning reds should stand in heaven
While the vesture of thy body slipped away
Black grief discolor all the woods
Night set gentle sail to shroud the sea

Nameless sorrow builds from stars a monument
Unto thy gaze upon the vault of heaven
And darkness bars with fortress wall

Light which looms from the new spring
The season peers in the still patterning of
Stars out from the cistern mirror of thy death.

03

Du selige Geburt wie tief verschwiegen
Entstieg ich ihm und war zur Stund bestimmt
Zu sein wie Nacht die ihm im Auge glimmt
Dem Leisesten auf weiten Himmelsstiegen

Der Strahl zu sein den er im Blick vernimmt
An welchem glücklich Ungeborne liegen
Mich inniger der Wange anzuschmiegen
Die im Azur als glühe Wolke schwimmt

Geschrieben stand daß nimmer sich beschwinge
Mein Mund wenn nicht in seinem Lied er stiege
Mein Haupt war nur ein letztes in dem Ringe

Der lodernd säumte mit Gebet die Wiege
Wie ist geschehen daß er mir entschwand
Führt meinen jungen Tod auf seiner Hand.

Thou blessed Birth how deeply silent I
arose from him was in that hour made
To be as night which glimmers in the eye
For him who softest treads the stairs of Heaven

Was made to be that beam his gaze perceives
On which are lying happy unborn beings
And press myself more inwardly against his cheek
Which swims the azure as a glowing cloud

So was it written: Never shall my mouth
Find eloquence if not aloft his song
My head was but a last one in the ring

A seam of flaming prayer about his cradle
How comes it that he disappeared for me
My young death he leads upon his hand.

04

Es waren seine Blicke im Erwachen
Mein einzig Leuchten auf den irren Fährten
Und seiner Augen Sterne sie gewährten
Den einzigen Schein in meinen Schlafgemachen

Nun sind dahingegangen die Gefährten
Die stummen Spiegel allen Geistes brachen
In diesen Himmeln die ihr feuchtes Lachen
Mit jedem Morgen seliger veklärten

Noch wenn sie weinten standen sie wie Lachen
Die sich im Fall der schweren Tropfen nährten
Und länger duften als die Regen währten

Und aus der Fülle ihrer Tränen sprachen
Die Dinge denen Namen noch gebrachen
Auf solche Art wie Blätter in den Gärten.

Waking were his glances my sole light
For errant traces and the starlight
Of his eyes the only beam
Bestowed upon my sleeping places

Now such companions are no more
Mute did the mirrors of all Spirit shatter
In these heavens which their glistening laugh
More blessedly transfigured with each morrow

Even when they wept they stood as pools
Themselves to nourish by the fall of heavy drops
Whose fragrance would outlast the shower

And in the fullness of their tears
Would those things speak which yet lacked names
Much as leaves may speak in gardens.

05

Du nie mehr klingende die in die Schwüle
Der grünen Hänge tauend niederschlug
In ihren Flügeln Windessingen trug
Dich machte stumm der Engel der Gefühle

O Stimme der mit seiner Hand erhub
Dein Atmen in die ewig klare Kühle
Wo deine Quelle nun am seligen Bühle
Jubelnden Mut verströmt nach Gottes Fug

Erwachet Vogelsang am grauen Morgen
Und fragt nach der Geliebten Aufenhalt
Er ahnt dich in dem stillen Licht geborgen

Das jugendlich die Buchen überwallt
Bis Mittag wo dein Wort dereinst geweilt
Den Leib der Stummen bricht den Stunden teilt.

Thou soundless now forever who didst drop
Thy dews into the sultry green of sloping hills
And in their byways bore the singing of the wind
The angel of emotions made thee dumb

O Voice he with his hand did lift thy breath
Into coolness clear and without end
Where presently upon the blessed hill thy spring
Streams forth its joy in keeping with God's will

Should birdsong waken in the gray of dawn
And ask where does the Loved One keep herself
It will thee sheltered know inside still light

Which wells up youthfully about the beeches
Til midday where thy word once lingered
Breaks the body of the Silent One divides it for the hours.

06

Da schon in hohen Schmerzensmeer verloren
Die Woge deines Lebens rollt vergib
Das scheue Lied das sehr verlaßne Lieb
Verschüttet aus dem leisen Mund der Toren

Das im vergeßnen Finster als ein Dieb
An Schlüften des Gebirgs das dich geboren
Zur Zinne irret ob die tauben Ohren
Dein Wehn erlauschteten im Windestrieb

Weinend daß dereinst du zur gütgen Stunde
Dich neigest seinem Reim und wehen Glanz
Ihm leihst vom Sange aus dem heißen Munde

Da du noch flochtest herber Strophen Kranz
Eh den entblätterten aus bleichen Wogen
Der Totengott ins schwarze Haar gebogen.

Even now thy life's great wave rolls lost
Upon high seas of hurt and so forgive
The most abandoned sweetheart his shy song
Spilled from the murmuring mouth of fools

Who wanders the forgotten darkness as a thief
By chasms in those ranges which did bear thee
Erring to the parapet where his deaf ears
Might hear thy birth pangs in the driving wind

Weeping that one day upon a friendly hour
Thou shouldst listen to his rhyme and lend him
Painful glory from the singing of thy burning mouth

For yet thou wove a wreath of bitter strophes
Before the God of Death did bind his leafless one
Of pallid waves into thy raven hair.

07

Wie soll mich dieses Tages Glänzen freuen
Wenn du nicht mit mir in die Wälder trittst
Wo Sonne in den schwarzen Ästen blitzt
Die konnte einst dein tiefer Blick erneuen

Indes der Lehre Wort dein Finger ritzt
In meines Denkens Tafel die in Treuen
Die Zeichen wahrte—und den Blick den scheuen
Erhebe ich doch wach am Wegrand sitzt

Der Tod statt deiner und ich bin im Walde
Verlassener als Busch und Baum zur Nacht
Ein Wind fährt über die entblößte Halde

Des Mittags Helle die mich jäh umfacht
Scheint vom gewölbten Himmel tiefer blauer
Wie eines rätselvollen Auges Trauer.

How should I joy in this day's gleaming
Comest thou with me not into the woods
Where through black branches sunlight flashes
Which thy piercing gaze once could renew

All while the teaching word thy finger etches
On the tablet of my thought
Loyal keeper of the runes—I lift my gaze shy gaze
Yet by the path sits wakeful

Death not thee and in the forest am I
More forsaken than are bush and tree at night
A wind fares past the empty hill

The midday blaze erupts all round me
From the vault of heaven deeper bluer shines
Like sorrow from an unrevealing eye.

08

Mein Leben sieh in deinem Schutz erlichtet
Der schon bereit aus Liebe zu gewähren
Als deine Mutter litt dich zu gebähren
Da war der Geist der sich in ihr verdichtet

Derselbe der in sommerlichen Ähren
Die Schöne seines Hauptes schwarz errichtet
Des bittre Stimme winters mich bezichtet
Vor dessen Anblick fließen meine Zähren

In deinem Leib mein Lieben ist gemeißelt
Und alle Wesen sind darin beseelet
Die vor dir stehen Kind die unverhehlet

Aus Wunden bluten die die Welt gegeißelt
Mir aber ist basalmischer gewesen
Als Basalm du aus welchem sie genesen

O see my life made bright with thy protection
Which to grant its light was ready out of love
So soon thy mother bearing thee did bear her pain
Then was the Spirit which condensed in her

The same which does in wheaten summer ears
To blackness build the beauty of his head
Whose bitter voice chastizes me in winter
And beneath whose gaze my tears do flow

In thy body is my loving chiseled
And therein ensouléd are all those
Who stand before thee as a child

Bleeding openly from wounds inflicted by the world
Yet more than balsam has been balm to me
Thyself through whom they healing find.

09

Verließe Nacht das innere Gemäuer
Das Euch verweilt zu lindem Aufenthalt
Den blinden Bann zersprengte die Gestalt
Euch winkt dem Gruße der Verblichnen teuer

Und Blumen springen auf im braunen Wald
Darinnen lodert das beseelte Feuer
Der Angst entfliegend aller Tage neuer
Unsterblichkeit ums Haupt Gewölke ballt

Auf feuchter Aue Euer Antlitz breitet
Für Helden Ruhe die sich süß verschwärmten
Wo die beflügelte Erinnrung schreitet

Die Dunkelheit den lauschenden Verhärmten
Die Melodie versinkt im Blau gespiegelt
Doch näher Land vom Morgenrot entsiegelt.

Were Night to leave the inner walls
Which linger for Your gentle stopping-place
Then Form would detonate the sightless spell
Greetings beckon for You from the dear departed

And blooms spring open in the autumn wood
Wherein is blazing the ensouléd fire
Fleeing dread with each new day
Immortality does cluster clouds about the head

For heroes sweetly scattered in their swarming
Your countenance spreads ease upon the watered green
Where winged memory finds its stride

Darkness for the careworn and their heedful ears
The melody is sinking mirrored in the blue
Yet unseals a closer land from out of morning red.

10

Wenn mich besuchtest du in meinem Leben
Es wird für dich nur leichte Mühe sein
Als trätest du wie einst ins Zimmer ein
Die nahe Schwelle winkt dir still und eben

Da wagte ich das Wort: o wär ich dein
Und also innig ward dir umgegeben
Mein Dasein gleich den leichtesten Geweben
Daß du's gewährtest denn du bliebst allein

Nur Raum ist um dich für ein Volk geworden
Seit du um dich die letzte Sehnsucht stillst
In einem Puls verschmelzen Süd und Norden

Und alles ist geschehen wie du willst
Mich suchst du nicht um dich nicht will ich weinen
Vor deinen Schein vergangen ist mein Scheinen.

When thou dost visit me within my life
It shall for thee but make the slightest trouble
A step as thou didst take before to enter in my room
The nearby threshold beckons still and even

Then might I dare to say: O could I but be thine
And by my Being wert thou thus enclosed
Wrapped round and round with such light webbing
Thou wouldst consent for yet thou wert alone

But round thee there is room to house a people
Since round thee thou dost still the last desire
Within one pulse melt South and North

And all is done in keeping with thy will
Me thou shalt not seek nor I weep for thee
Before thy shining has my seeming vanished.

11

Einst war die weiße Stadt von seinen Schritten
Wie Sang erfüllt in ihren Fenstern starb
Sein Blick gespiegelt und das Aug verbarg
Vor ihm der Tag in stumpfer Himmel Mitten

Die sengend hingen über altem Park
Wo ihn im Wellenschlag gewährter Bitten
Schlummer umfloß dess grüne Flut entglitten
Dem Born der Sonnen als ihn heimlich stark

Engel entrückten in die fernsten Länder
Verschneiter Berge wo der Freundin Atem
Hernieder wehte linnene Gewänder

Den Knaben hüllten schimmernder Granaten
Gebüsch sich beugte übers müde Haupt
Vom Strahle ewgen Monds die Stirn umlaubt.

As though with song was once the white town
with his footsteps filled his gaze turned back
Within its windows died and Day did hide
From him its eye amid the sullen sky

Which scorching overhung the ancient park
Where in the wave-ring made by granted wishes
Sleep did round him flow a green flood scaping
From the font of suns when he by angels was

With furious stealth removed to furthest lands
Of mountains sunk in snow whence his lady's breath
Sent linen garments fluttering down to shroud

The youth a bush of gleaming bombshells
Bent itself above his listless head
The moon eternal wreathes his brow with beams.

12

Einst wird von dem Gedenken und Vergessen
Nichts bleiben als ein Lied an seiner Wiege
Das nichts verriete und nichts verschwiege
Wortloses Lied das Worte nicht ermessen

Ein Lied das aus dem Grund der Seele stiege
Wie aus der Erde Winden und die Kressen
Wie Stimmen in den Orgtelton der Messen
In dieses Lied sich unser Hoffen schmiege

Kein Trost kann außer diesem Liede leben
Und keine Traurigkeit fern von dem Lied
Darin sind Stern und Tier wie in Geweben

Und Tod und Freunde ohne Unterschied
In diesem Lied lebt ein jedes Ding
Dieweil der Schritt des Schönsten in ihm ging.

One day remembrance and forgetting will but be
A song around his cradle and no more
With nothing to lay bare and nothing to conceal
 A wordless song words cannot measure

A song ascending from the bottom of the Soul
As from the earth do weeds and watercresses
As voices enter in the organ tone of Masses
Into this song let our hopes nestle

This song outside of which no solace lives
And far from which no sorrow
Within are star and beast together woven

Nor death nor friends are told apart
Within this song lives each and every thing
So long as in it went his step most beautiful of men.

13

Zu spät erwachte unser müdes Schauen
Da Abendwolken purpurn schon beschatten
Das Sinken jener Stirn die ohn Ermatten
Umworben unser zagendes Vertrauen

So muß sich Andacht mit dem Tode gatten
Der trägt sie auf verschwiegner Fahrt den grauen
Wildnissen zu und blassen Lorbeerauen
Den Wassern welche in den leisen glatten

Wellen sein Wort sich singen und Gedanken
Dort überhängend sieht am Wolkensaum
Die Waage des Gerichts er sonder Schwanken

Zu ihm geneigt indessen seinen Traum
Die flehenden Gedächtnisse bewegen
Der nimmermehr sie stillt mit Trost noch Segen.

Too late our weary watch did wake
When evening clouds had thrown their purple veil
Across the sinking of that brow which never
Wearied in its courtship of our doubtful trust

Across the sinking of that brow which never
Tired in its courtship of our doubtful trust
Of gray and meads of palest myrtle
To waters in whose soft smooth waves

His words are sung as well his thoughts
Extending there from hem of cloud he sees
The scales of judgment bend to favor him

Straightway while pleading memories
Do his dream quicken which shall never
Quiet them with solace or with blessing.

14

Ich bin im Bunde mit der alten Nacht
Und wurde alt von ihr nicht unterschieden
Hat Traurigkeit im Herzen ohne Frieden
Die Herdstatt ihrer Schatten angefacht

Was so entfernte Not zu Einer macht
Die sonnenlose irdische hienieden
Und mein Verfinstern das der Freund gemieden
Das habe ich im Wachen oft bedacht

In solcher Nacht ist Schlafen mehr denn selten
Dem Schlummerlosen schenkt sie ihre Helle
Die könnte nicht für Tag den Menschen gelten

Und doch bestrahlt sie seine wahren Welten
Kein andres Licht blüht ja auf seiner Schwelle
Erinnerung sein Mond und sein Geselle.

I am in league with ancient Night
Grown old with nothing to distinguish us
And in my restless heart has sorrow
Fanned the home place of her shadows

Making such unlike distresses into One
The sunless trouble here below on earth
And that eclipse of me which my friend shunned
By waking often have I thought of it

In such a night is slumber more than rare
She sends the sleepless one her light
Which could not serve mankind for day

Yet turns its ray on his true worlds
No other light will bloom upon his threshold
Memory his moon and his bedfellow.

15

Die Jahre sind nun nicht mehr wie die Wogen
Wenn sie das Meerschiff senken oder heben
Ich bin der Steuermann am ruhigen Leben
Des Schiffes Segelwald hat mich betrogen

Ich habe ihn am Tage eingezogen
Als sich der gute Wind in ihm gegeben
Die weite Fläche ward unnennbar eben
Und hat Vergangnes unter mir erwogen

Die Spiegelwelt in ihren blassen Farben
Erging sich im Verwandeln ohne Lust
Ich wendete mich nieder zu dem Blust

Und fahndete in seinen feuchten Garben
Erinnerungen nach die bald verdarben
Im Wellenbild des blendenden August.

No longer do the years resemble waves
When they draw down or lift an ocean vessel
I am steersman on the placid life
A trick the flock of sails did play on me

Which I took in upon that day
A goodly wind was filling them
Calm past naming went the broad face of the sea
To ponder things past under me

The mirror world in its pale hues
Did give itself to transformation without joy
Stooping to the water-bloom

I searched its dripping sheaves
For memories which soon found ruin
Inside the wave-ring of deceiving August.

16

Die um dich klagen den Zeilen von Sehnsucht und Leid
Schenke das silberne Maß und des Geistes Erwarten
Wie Erwarten reifender Frucht dem Baume im Garten
Wie Winters Erwarten der herbstlichen Traurigkeit

Und dem trägen Vergessen unabwendbarem harten
Gib Schlaf du Erbarmer in sinkender Zeit
Und lege die Hand die der Tod dir geweih
Auf weinende Augen zum Teppich der zarten

Und wecke den Morgen mit deinem Gewissen
Und wiege den Mittag auf deinem Arm
Und heile die Stimme von Tränen zerissen

Und wehre dem bösen und lästernden Harm
Und lebe im Innern von Stunde zu Stunde
Empfangend der Seele verzehrende Funde.

To verses which lament thee those of pain and longing
Dispense the silver measure and a waiting for the Spirit
So to orchard tree the wait for ripening fruit
So to autumn sorrowing the wait for winter

And to slow forgetting harsh and ineluctable
Give sleep O thou who pities in the sinking time
And lay the hand which Death has blessed for thee
On weeping eyes for tender eyes a cover

And wake the morning with thy conscience
And rock the midday on thy arm
And heal the voice all torn with tears

And fend against blaspheming wicked grief
And live within me hour after hour
Taking to thee findings which consume the Soul.

17

Die Harfe hängt im Wind sie kann nicht wehren
Daß deines Todes Hauch die Saiten rührt
Der in den Herzen große Feuer schürt
Und Wellen lächeln macht auf hohen Meeren

Zur frühen Stunde da du mich entführt
Gedenkst du noch der silbernen Galeeren
Des glühenden Gespräches eh in Schären
Die feuchten Dünste deine Stirn berührt

Kann nun verwehter Hauch dich noch erreichen
Da schon die Wolke deinen Blick umfängt
Und lauschst du noch dem trauervollen Zeichen

Das sich im nächtgen Winde zu dir drängt
Den Klang vernimmst du den ersterbend warfen
Im letzten Schmerz zerspringend meine Harfen.

The harp hangs in the wind it cannot hinder
That the exhalation of thy death shall touch its strings
That breath which stirs large fires inside hearts
And causes waves to frolic on high seas

At the early hour thou didst make me captive
Dost remember still the silver galleys
Of our glowing talk before thy brow has grazed
Thick fogs in stony islets off the shore

Can breath dispersed yet find its way to thee
When cloud already swathes thy gaze
Dost still harken to the sorrowing sign

Which to thee presses in the nocturn wind
Discern the sound which my expiring harps
Threw out while breaking under their last grief.

18

In seine Hände mocht ich meine Stunden
Wie Knospen schütten die um ihn erblühn
Gedachte mit des Schweigens Immergrün
Die Stirn zu schirmen die Gesänge runden

Ihm sollte meines Armes Schwertschlag glühn
Im Kampfe der gebenedeiten Wunden
Wo sich Verrat auf seinen Pfad gewunden
Mein Warnen sollte wie Fanfaren sprühn

Ich wollte Schild sein dem erwählten Ritter
Daß er durch helle Wälder müßig streife
Sein Bote wär mein Mund das süßt was bitter

Weht atmend daß ihn Winter nicht bereife
Dies alles tat er mir nicht ich tat's ihm
Zu Füßen liegt er nun gelöst den Riem.

Into his hands I wished to pour my hours
Like unto flower buds which should about him bloom
And with the evergreen of silence did I think
To shade his brow to round his songs

For his sake should the sword-stroke of my arm
In battle burn for dearly blessed wounds
And where'er was treason wound along his path
My warning should like fanfares fly

A shield were I to serve the chosen knight
To let him roam through shining woods at ease
My mouth his herald to sweeten what is bitter

And breathe warm breath lest winter cover him in frost
All this he did for me not I for him
Who at my feet now lies and all undone.

19

Nur eine Stunde hat der Geist geweiht
In seinem Namen wenn die ernsten Frühen
Mit ihrem Licht den Osten übersprühen
Und regen Winden Venus gibt Bescheid

Dann tauchet aus den Händen sonder Mühen
Der dunklen Röte stumme Heiterkeit
Und ein verfrühter Strahl der jüngsten Zeit
Steht in den Augen welche nicht mehr glühen

Die werden uns den Morgen nie entzünden
Der um die Dächer allzuhelle kragt
Zur Stunde nur steigt aus den Blumengründen

Erwachter West der seine Schwinge wagt
Und von dem Duft der Hyazinthen trunken
Den Flüchtenden verfolgt der schon versunken.

One hour only has the Spirit consecrated
In his name when break of day
Does gently wash the East in sober light
And Venus gives her order to the stirring winds

Then shall mute sky of dim dark red
Emerge unlabored from the hands
And from time's end a beam untimely
In eyes stand which no longer shine

No more shall they for us the morning kindle
Which all too brightly stands about the roofs
There is only rising out of beds in flower

Zephyrus waked who will his pinions try
And drunk with perfume of the hyacinth
Pursue the fugitive already sunk from view.

20

Vergängnis bebt in den Beseelten allen
Wie Tanz verblieb im Herz des Tänzers stet
Ob auch die Geige schwieg zur Heimkehr spät
Begleiten Wolken ihn in Wälderhallen

Vernehmt zur Einkehr aller Wesen lädt
Sein Tod der wächst gleich ästigen Korallen
Den unermeßnen Nächten zu Gefallen
Ist er erwählt zum köstlichen Gerät:

Das Szepter Seliger die nicht ermüden
Der Leib den nicht mehr Zeitlichkeit zerbricht
Ist wie das Kreuz das Sterne über Süden

Gezeichnet haben als ein Maß und Richt
So halten ihn die Götter nun in Händen
Weil der verlacht wird den sie lebend senden.

Pastness quivers inside all who are ensouled
So dance remained within the dancer's heart
Even though the bow fell silent late on homeward way
Clouds companion him in sounding woodland halls

See how it invites the turning in of all
His death which grows like richly branching coral
And to please the nights illimitable
He is chosen for a precious implement:

A scepter of the bless'd who do not tire
His body which time passing rends no more
Is as the Cross which stars have drawn

Above the South for guide and measure
Now the gods shall keep him in their hands
For whom they send alive is ridiculed and mocked.

21

Als mich die Stimme rief die nächtens spricht
Ward ich wie Sterbende ins Schiff entrissen
In Segeln meinen trügerischen Kissen
Verwähnte ich geborgen mein Gesicht

Vor ihm der kommt im Wind und kommt mit Wissen
Die schwarze Woge netzt ihn sicher nicht
Er birgt in seiner Brust das bloße Licht
Das ihm verliehen aus den Finsternissen

Die über Nacht um meine Seele werben
Wenn sich die träge Seele vor dem Herrn ziert
Und sich allabendlich ins Nichts verliert

In solcher Zeit soll sie um ihn verderben
Jedoch aus ihm der ihren Tag gebiert
Ist sie erwacht und wußte sich im Sterben.

Summoned by that voice which speaks at night
I was as are the dying dragged into the ship
Within its sails my trickster cushion
I did falsely dream my face secure

From him who comes in wind and comes with knowing
The black wave surely wets him not
He stores sheer light within his breast
Light lent him out of darknesses

Which through the night vie for my sluggish Soul
When coyly she presents herself before the Lord
As often she does lose herself in nothingness

Then for sake of him my Soul shall perish
Yet from him who did give birth unto her day
Being waked she knew that she was dying.

22

Ihr meine Lippen wollt Euch stumm erzeigen
Und ungeheilt verharschen? o der Wunde
Die nie mehr purpurn wie zur Schwertesstunde
Sich öffnet lasset denn ins Schwert mich steigen

Will Klage ohne Maß aus meinem Munde
Sich nicht mehr schütten der dem Freunde eigen
So ward vorm Tode heillos auch das Schweigen
Mit seinem Sein ist ja mein Schmerz im Bunde

Nicht ehe späte eh gereifte Frühe
Aus seinen jungen Jahren überflutet
Und seiner Sterbestunde leichte Mühe

Weltmorgen rötet weil er von ihr blutet
Wird meiner Schmerzen hohe Flut gestillt
Zum ebnen Meer des Aufgangs Spiegelbild.

Wish You my lips to make a show of muteness
And to seal yourselves unhealed? O for the wound
Which never more its crimson gapes as in the hour
Of the sword upon the blade then let me sink

If measureless lamenting no more spills
Forth from my mouth which is my friend's
Before his death the silence too grew hopeless
In truth my pain is bound up with his Being

Until the late nay ripened morn
Shall overspill from his young years
Until the easy effort of his dying hour

Makes red the world-morn which does bleed from it
Unbroken be the high tide of my sorrow
Falling not to even sea the mirror of his rising.

23

Nun ist der Schleier weggezogen
Ich blicke so ins Herz der Welt
Wie wir nicht sollen Unverstellt
Sah ich das Feuer darin wogen

Da mich vom Widerschein umflogen
Die ewige Flamme die erhellt
Mit einem kühlen Hauch befällt
Fühl ich mich innerlich betrogen

Ich war versunken anzuschauen
Ein Feuer das sich selbst verhüllt
Das Weltall unter seinen Brauen

Mein Schicksal hat sich nicht erfüllt
Geblendet droh ich zu vergessen
Sein Leben das mir zugemessen.

Now is the curtain fully parted
And I peer inside the world's heart
As we ought not   Without disguise
I saw the fire surging there

When round me glimmers fly
And by the flame eternal I am struck
Which sheds its light with cooling breath
Then inwardly I feel deceived

I was absorbed to contemplate
A fire which did hide itself
The universe beneath his brows

My fate has missed of its fulfilling
Dazzled I am tempted to forget
His life which was assigned to me.

24

Uns jüngsten Tages wird der Gott entfachen
Goldnes Gespräch erneut darin die Dinge
Sich flüsternden Geräts auf Silberschwinge
Begegnen wie Losruf treuer Wachen

Dichtender Schweigsamkeit verwehrtem Ringe
Der brüderlichen Ahnung Lippen sprachen
Nächtigt in Schluchten des Olympos Lachen
Betenden Scherz darin das All erklinge

Noch Worte in den gleichen Schalen schwankten
Die spät Vertrauen auf den Händen stillte
Vor nahen Todesmalen am erkrankten

Lüsternen Fluche stürzen die Gebilde
Weil frühe Sterne überm Haupte glimmen
Und Eros' Traubenmund in unsern Stimmen.

Golden converse shall the Lord ignite for us
On the Last Day when all things now renewed
Shall meet with whisper-instruments on silver wings
As does the faithful watchmen's word

That proscribed ring who make up poems of silence
Lips of brotherly foreknowing spoke
Laughter spends the night in chasms of Olympos
Their prayerful jest in which the universe should sing

Words yet swayed in equal scales which late
Were quieted by trusting on the hands
Before approaching signs of death

Structures lapse from sickly lustful curses
All while above us early stars are gleaming
And within our voices Eros's breath of wine.

[25]

Dies eingeschnitten rosigem Karneole
Erblickt ich dessen Härte nicht ertrüge
Das laute Sagen eine Flucht nein Flüge
Von Wagenlenkern Rossen welches hole

Den Ölzweig und im Kampf die Brüder schlüge
Die Kehr die strahlig gleich der Aureole
Aufglüht im Steine daß sich wiederhole
Die Palmenbahn trug Sommer im Gefüge

So kenn ich andern Kampf der streng in Zucht hält
Mein Tod und Leben sind die Renner beide
Und dies der Preis aus dem ein tiefer Duft fällt

Daß nie mein Tod ganz sonder Süße leide
Mein schneller Herbst der heimlich auf der Flucht hält
Du bist der Herr und Knabe der die Frucht hält.

This I did glimpse carved in the rosy carnelian
Whose hardness would not bear a spoken telling
A fleeing o nay flights of chariot riders
Steeds the one who bears away the olive

Branch in fighting overwhelms the brothers
The turn which shining like an aureole
Begins to glow inside the stone and makes
The palm-path two held summer in its fabric

So know I another match which keeps me well in hand
My Death and Life are they who run
And this the prize which drops its heady scent

That never shall my Death all without sweetness suffer
O my rapid Autumn who in fleeing makes his secret halt
Thou art both master and the boy who holds the fruit.

26

Der jungen Ewigkeit geliebte Kinder
Hat Tod in seine Wälder fortgetragen
Staunender lag ihr Auge aufgeschlagen
In beiden gleichen Blicken welche linder

Als je erglühten in sterblichen Tagen
Weil Lieb demütig schwieg ob mehr ob minder
Im einen oder andern Überwinder
Irdischer Angst trug des Gesanges Wagen

Leid hing hernieder als gereifte Frucht
Von allen Zweigen über die Erinnern
Hinhauchte der genossnen Küsse Duft

Und waffenlose Engel vor dem Innern
Des Gartens hielten neuem Paradies
In das die freudenvolle Andacht wies.

Into his woods has Death them borne away
Beloved children of the young eternity
With more amaze their eyes did open wide
In two like looks which softer shone

Than ever in the mortal days
While Love fell humbly silent whether more or less
And in one or in the other vanquisher
Of earthly anguish bore the van of song

Down sorrow hung as ripened fruit
From all and every branch while Memory above
Forth breathed the perfume of past sweet kisses

And angels without weapons stood before
The inner garden a new Paradise
Into which joyful Reverence showed the way.

27

Wie grosse Winde segelschwellend warm
Ziehn durch die Lande hin die Feiertage
Die Kinder spielen durch die hellen Hage
Und Mahd hält Todes unermüdter Arm

Du arme Sehnsucht wo erklingt die Sage
Von den Gefeierten der Glockenschwarm
Wen fugt er frühe und der Kinder Harm
Wer stillt ihn und die gelle Totenklage

Da die Gefeierten und die Geliebten
Die Sehenden und die Erbarmenden
Geschieden sind im abendlich getrübten

Licht glitten hin die sich Umarmenden
Zum Hades wo der Seele Ort bereitet
Vor ihrem Blick der glüht und der geleitet.

Like great winds warm and swelling of the sail
Holidays go wandering across the land
Playful children thread the shining hedges
And Death's untiring arm does mow

Thou poor Yearning say where sounds the tale
Of those remembered whom do swarming bells
Too soon unite the children's grief who stills it
And the shrill lamenting for the dead

Now that those remembered and those loved
Those who see and those who pity
Are departed embracing they did glide

Their way in dreary evening light to Hades
Where a seat is readied for the Soul
Before their gaze which glows and follows.

28

So leis verläßt uns nicht der goldne Mond
Wenn ihn die erste Morgenwolke säumt
So sanft nicht Woge überm Strande bäumt
Nicht Westwind so mit lauen Munde lohnt

Den Wipfel der Zypresse und es träumt
Inniger atmend nicht die Braut gewohnt
Als in der blinden Mitternacht die thront
Dies schwüle Leben Euer Haupt geräumt

Die ohne Leid und Säumnis Ihr den Gang
Den längst erlosten rietet früh im Glück
Noch zu beginnen der Euch je gelang

Nie überlegen Lied und Freund zurück
Wie Wandrer der am nahen Hügel ruht
Entferntes schaut weil langer Schlaf ihn lud.

The golden moon forsakes us not so gently
Having found its fringe of early morning cloud
So softly never looms the wave above the strand
Ever West wind so mild of mouth its boon bestow

On cypress-tip nor dreams with more
Contented breath the well-accustomed bride
Than did Your heads breathe out this fetid life
Beneath blind midnight's triumph

You who without anguish or delay did choose
The way long fated who still happy did soon take
The path which always brought good fortune

Friend and song will never think You back
So a wanderer who rests upon the hill close by
Will look on distant things because invited to long slumber.

29

Du Schlummender doch Leuchte des Erwachens
Trauriger du doch der Betrübten Tröster
Verstummter dennoch Jubelruf Erlöster
Weinender du heilender Gott des Lachens

Geleit der Einsamen du selbst ein grösster
Verlassener am Rand des Todesnachens
Der Liebe keuscher Herr und Rauschentfachens
Bote der Schönheit du in Not entblösster

Engel des Friedens den das Schwert zerschnitten
Bleühendes Kind des Todes Spielgeselle
Retter der winkt aus der Vernichtung Mitten

Beter vertrieben von der tauben Schwelle
Ergreister Götter Bringer neuer Huld
Sei Heiland du und Löser unsrer Schuld

Thou slumberer yet lamp for waking
Sorrower thou yet comforter to those who grieve
One silenced yet who frees the joyous shout
Weeps and is the healing god of laughter

Escorter of the lonely thou so greatly
Desolate thyself beside the skiff of Death
Chaste lord of love of kindled passion
Messenger of beauty thou who art reduced to want

Angel of peace dismembered by the sword
Blooming child Death's playmate
Rescuer who beckons us from deep within destruction

Prayer driven from unhearing thresholds
Of gray gods bringer of new grace
Be thou our Deliverer redeem our guilt.

30

Entstiege deine Hand zum letztenmale
Dem Grab und neige sich zu meinem Worte
Sieh dann erblühte wohl der schon verdorrte
Mein Sang und Tränen sprengten ihre Schale

In deiner Hände freudenvolle Orte
Drängten des Liedes farbige Fanale
Wie Falter aus dem abgeblühten Tale
Der Seele steigen die des Südens Horte

Sehnsüchtig suchen immer wieder wagen
Sie ihren Flug der sie ins Irre führt
Aus Hoffnung zu den späten Sommertagen

Wo dunkler Blumen Saft in Kelche schürt
Vielleicht ersteht noch rot empor gewendet
Ein Asternkelch der keinen Duft mehr spendet.

Should thy hand arise but one last time
And leave the grave to lend itself unto my word
Behold so might my song the dessicated
Bloom my tears their casings sunder

And iridescent beacons of my music
Crowd into the joyous places of thy hands
As butterflies lift from the withered vale
Which is the Soul's and yearning seek the shelter

Of the South forever and again they try
Their flight that leads them far astray with hope
Of reaching final summer days where sap

Still smolders in the chalice of dark flowers
Yet rising red and turning to the sky may be
An aster's cup which breathes its scent no more.

31

Von Sonne lauter eine Zeit wird sein
Wir Lauschenden erkennen sie am Sang
Der heißen Winde und am Überschwang
Des Sturms in dem sich Schmetterlinge freien

An langen Tagen wird uns nicht mehr bang
Um Schwestern im verweilenden Verein
Auftaucht kein Abend überm schwarzen Rain
Und Herbst und Winter haben keinen Gang

Es weiß der Boden selbst von seinem Schritt
Nicht mehr und von der Stimme sein die Luft
Sein Name keinem Freundesmund entglitt

Und nie mehr Liebende dem Schläfer ruft
Der in den vielchenfarbenen Gewanden
Um Mittag bei uns war und auferstanden.

Of pure sunlight there shall be a time
Which we who harken are to know
From singing of the torrid winds and from the brimful
Storm in which are wooing butterflies

Long days over we shall no more fear
For sisters drawing out their trysts
No evening show above the blackened ridge
And fall and winter find a way in

The very ground shall know his step no more
And of his voice no more the air
From no friend's mouth escaped his name

No more shall lover call the sleeping one
He who with us was at noon in garb
Of violets' hue and who is risen.

[32]

Mir wahrt der Tag aus seinem Licht die Gnade
Der letzten Stunde die mit Gold verbrämt
Den Saum der Wolke wenn sich müd gegrämt
Verlassene Erinnerung zum Bade

Der hellen Wasser beuget sich verschämt
Der Geist am Weiher wo die braunen Pfade
Von Freundestritten führen in die grade
Unendlichkeit die meine Sinne lähmt

Und ich erkenne den bereiten Ort
Mein Fuss hält ein das Gras soll unversehrt
Der Boden heil verbleiben mich belehrt

Der schräge Strahl der Sonne welche dort
Dem Horizonte ihre Glut beschert:
Der Tag verscheidet mir erscheint mein Hort.

Day grants me from its light the blessing
Of the final hour when it fills with gold
The fringe of cloud and Memory forsaken
Will have worn herself with grieving chastely

Stoops the Spirit to his bath of shining
Waters by the pond where earthen
Paths of my friend's stepping lead to
Endlessness unbending numbing to the senses

And I recognize the ready place
My foot ceases unharmed the grass
Unfazed the ground shall be a slant

Of sun which lends its fire to far distant
Sky reveals to me this lesson:
Day is dying my refuge lies ahead.

33

In Gott eröffne ich mein Testament
Und hinterlasse meiner Tochter Liebe
Wenn meine Zeit verronnen wie im Siebe
Wasser verrint wie Reisig niederbrennt

Hier dieses Buch das sie von jung auf kennt
Warum ich es bis in den Tod verschiebe
Ihr auszuliefern was ihr ewig bliebe
Hat diesen Grund: wenn uns die Stunde trennt

Mein Leib verfällt von Sehnsucht aufgezehrt
Dies überdauert dessen Blätter Reben
Verschliessen die kein Wachstum je vermehrt

Dann will ich es im Sterben übergeben
An meiner Tochter Liebe die es wert
Dass jubelnd sie's erkenne als sein Leben.

In God I do make known my testament
And hereby leave unto my daughter Love
So soon my time is run as water runs
Across the sieve as brushwood burns to ash

This book which she has known from youngest years
Why do I wait until my death shall come
To yield to her what should stay hers forever
Here then is my reason: When the Hour parts us

And my body falls away with longing wasted
This shall survive whose leaves enclose such vines
As growth may never multiply the more

So in dying let me relinquish it
Unto my worthy daughter Love
That she may joy and know it was his life.

34

Ich saß am Abend über mich gebeugt
Und um mich regte sich dein süßes Leben
Der Spiegel meines Geistes blickte eben
Als hättest du aus seinem Grund geäugt

Da dachte ich von dir bin ich gesäugt
In deinen Atem will ich mich ergeben
Denn deine Lippen hangen wie die Reben
Und haben stumm vom Innersten gezeugt

Es ist mein Freund dein Dasein mir entwunden
Ich taste wie der Schläfer nach dem Kranz
Im eignen Haar nach dir in dunklen Stunden

Doch war dein Mantel einmal wie im Tanz
Um mich getan und aus dem schwarzen Rund
Dein Antlitz riß den Odem mir vom Mund.

I sat one night to ponder on myself
And round me thy sweet life did stir
The mirror of my mind glanced back
As hadst thou just looked out from in its depths

Then came the thought: Thou sucklest me
Into thy breath I shall my self surrender
For like grapes hanging are thy lips
Which have mute witness borne to inmost things

O friend thy presence has been wrested from me
Like one asleep whose hand looks for the wreath
In his own hair so in dark hours I for thee

Though once thy cloak did round me go
As were there dancing and from within the midnight throng
Thy look did snatch the breath out of my mouth.

35

Ob ich den Freund so fragtest du mich liebe?
Also erlösend was sich jahrlang staute
In deiner Stimme welcher ich vertraute
Ihr Hauch zerschmelzte das Kristall der Triebe

In meiner Tränen wolkiges Geschiebe
Ihr Wort verwandelte die Brust zur Laute
Die unter deiner süßen Frage taute
Verstohlnes Ja daran ward ich zum Diebe

Doch meiner Lippe im Bekennen träge
Harrte ein Meister der sie besser präge
Die Hand die zagt ob sie dem Freund sich schenkt

Hat er ergriffen der sie härter lenkt
Daß sie das Herz das liebte im Geheimen
Nun aller Welt verschütten muß in Reimen.

And do I love—so didst thou ask—my friend?
Thus loosing what had knotted been
For years within thy trusted voice
Whose breath did melt the crystal of the drives

Into the cloudscape of my pressing tears
Whose word remade my breast a lute
Which to thy question sweet did thaw
A surreptitious "Yes"—I turned a thief.

But for my lips slow to confess a master
Waited who should better mark them
The hand which hesitates itself to give

To friend is by him seized a crueller guide
So that the heart which loved in secret
Must now be spilled for all to see in rhymes.

36

Wie flammte dieser Tage Hauch von Würzen
Die über dir geliebte Stadt erwachten
Und spät erst in Gewässern und in Schachten
Verglühend sanken hinter Giebelstürzen

Wenn über deinem grünen Mittag lachten
Die Schläge die einander nie verkürzen
Der Stunden so die Münsterglocken schürzen
Kam Rasten nach die Stadt begann das Nachten

Da schwieg das Laub und sang der Wein im Kelche
In Reden flüstert noch des Flusses Rauschen
Beim Freund wacht Freundschaft die nicht forschet welche

Gefühle leiser im Geliebten tauschen
Denn von der offnen Lippe weht sie fort
Das nächtlich haust bei Liebenden das Wort.

How flaming was the breath of days with scents
Which over you beloved town awoke
And only at the last behind your gable flights
Ceased glowing and did sink in waters and in wells

When high above your green noonday there laughed
The strikings which shall never shorten one another
Of those hours storing up the minster bells
Whereupon came rest the town began its night

Now trees fell silent and the wine in goblets sang
Inside our talk the rushing river whispers still
And in the friend a friendship wakes which does not guess

A quieter change of feeling in the loved one
For it blows away from open lips
That word which shelters every night with lovers.

37

Uns will die Stadt noch einmal eigen sein
Denn alles selge Glück ist Wiederkommen
Und wird wie Echo eines Walds vernommen
Dem viele Klüfte ihre Stimme leihn

Und dichte Stämme wurzelnd im Verein
Der klaren Bäche die den Wipfeln frommen
Dort fangen Äste die wie Kerzen glommen
Den äußern Tag um unsre Stirnen ein

Und es ermißt das Auge Schaft an Schaft
Erspäht im Laub das glimmende Gesicht
In bunten Scheiben brach sich solches Licht

Aus Krypten ragte so der Säule Kraft
Dort stand die Sonne im Zenith so finster
Und es ist wieder Mittag in dem Münster.

Ours the town once more will be
Returning brings each blessed joy
And shall but seem like echoes of a wood
To which the many chasms lend their cry

Like heavy trunks of trees with roots inside
A bright commingling of brooks to benefit the tips
There branches which did glow like tapers
Seize the outer day about our brows

The eye takes measure shaft on shaft
Espies in foliage the glimmer of a face
In panes of many tint such light did break

From crypts so rose the power of the columns
There stood the sun upon so dark a zenith
And once more it is midday in the minster.

38

Märkische Stadt und Marken sind verblaßt
Das Schneegeriesel trieb dich um du lebstest
Im Geist verschwiegen und im Worte bebtest
Wie Kiefernwipfel du die Frost erfaßt

Der Havelsee den du im Fliehn bewegtest
Betrachtete dein Abbild in dem Glast
Der hohen Fürstenstufen schwache Last
Schreitend im Stürzen Schuh du niederlegtest

Ein nördliches Gestirn war aufgestiegen
Am Sommertag den wir allein erkannten
Die Täler schwiegen in gewohnten Riegen

Geklärte Kuppen schwarz im Abend brannten
Das losch im dichten Haare dir versinkend
Und glimmt im Winter zauberischer winkend.

Gone white the marchland town and marches
Drizzling snow did drive thee all about thou livedst
In the stillness of thy mind in speaking thou didst
Quake like tips of firs that frost has seized

The Havelsee which thou didst stir in fleeing
Looked upon thine image in the gleaming light
The meager burden of high princely stairs
Striding in thy falling thou put down the shoe

A northern star had risen on the
Summer day which only we did know
The valleys kept their silence in accustomed ranks

Pure peaks burned black upon the evening
Sinking down the star expired in thy clustered hair
And glows in winter winking more enchantedly.

39

Wir Frühesten sind doch zu spät geflohn
Das Nahen zu ertragen vom Gericht
Vergingen unsre Kniee im Gewicht
Gefällt zu werden in der Prozession

Wir lebten damals wie im Pavillon
Und hatten miteinander Ein Gesicht
Wir nannten in dem Fenster gleiches Licht
Die Abendröte und das Morgenlohn

Wir alle liebten Einen unabwendlich
In dessen Liebe sich ein jedes wagte
Weil er ihm ferne hielt was schwach und schändlich

War unser Glück fast ausgereift und ländlich
Als ihn dahingerafft was uns verklagte
Und eine Welt entdeckte schlecht und endlich.

Even we earliest ones are flown too late
To bear the nearing of the Judgment
Our knees did buckle from the weight
Of being felled in the procession

Then we lived as in a pleasure garden
Together shared One single vision
One name did give the window-light
The red of evening and the morning flame

One we all did love steadfastly
And to love this man was each one bold
For what is weak and shameful he kept from us

Fair ripe unto perfection was our joy
When he was snatched away which did accuse us
And lay bare a mean and ending world.

40

Ich habe mich der Stunde heut entsonnen
Und auch das Lager fiel mir wieder bei
Auf dem mich fand vom Traume kaum erst frei
Der Horizont von Röte überronnen

Im Fenster stand die Dämmerung wie Blei
Von einem Tag der ehe er begonnen
Im Schlummer mir das Leben abgewonnen
In dunkler Brust riß er mein Herz entzwei

Und macht sich aus dem Staube dieser Zeit
Verblichen war der unheilvolle Morgen
Am Mittagshimmel welcher das Geleit

Bespiegelte in dem wir ihn geborgen
Der trübe Abend sprach mit Deutlichkeit
Von nun an muß dein Glück von frühern borgen.

Today I have recalled the hour and
To me came back as well the bed on which
I being from the dream but scarcely freed
Overrun with red the distant sky discovered me

The dawn like lead stood in my window
Dawn of that day which ere it was begun
Did wrest my life from me in sleep
In my dark breast did shear the heart in two

And hastes away in dust formed of this time
Faded was the catastrophic morning on the
Midday sky which showed the escort back to us

We made for him to be secure
The dismal evening spoke with no mistaking
Henceforth thy happiness must draw from happinesses past.

41

Höre Seele höre deiner harrt
Ein Tisch wie noch keinem bereitet ward
Einst läßt du dich sicher daran nieder
Mehr als ein Lager löset die Glieder

Der Schemel ist sein Holz auch hart
Dich entblößt der Gegenwart
Undurchsichtiges Gefieder
Abwärts blätterned hin und wieder

Was erfüllt dich aber ein
Duft der deinen Odem bauschet?
Deines Freundes voll wird sein

Auf dem Tisch der Becher Wein
Der dein Leben so berauschet
Daß es mit dem Tode tauschet.

Hear O Soul O hear on thee a table waits
Like none prepared till now for any other
Here surely shalt thou sit thee down one day
More than thy bed its stool though

Hard bare wood does soothe thy limbs
And of the Present thou art stripped
By veiling feathers which trail downward
Now and then like shedding leaves

Yet what is it fills thee
What perfume billows out thy breath?
The goblet on the table

Shall of thy friend be full
Wine which does so thrill thy life
It will with Death change places.

42

Die Stunden welche die Gestalt enthalten
Sind in dem Haus des Traumes abgelaufen
Und wir werden andre nicht erkaufen
Diese Nacht der bräutlichen Gewalten

Wie die Strahlen in den Fenstern raufen
Silbern schwirrt die Schwinge durch die Spalten
Meines Hauses Hof verging zum kalten
Mondenhofe mit den roten Traufen

Von Gestirn die diese Nacht kristallten
Stuben darf ich sieben nicht durchlaufen
Wo Planeten ihre Wache halten

Und sie werden mit dem Strahle taufen
Meine Stirne der in Schlafes Walten
Er entfacht ward jäh wie Fächerfalten.

Those hours which contain the Figure
Have expired in the house of dreams
And we shall gain no more of them
Upon this night of nuptial powers

While beams contend inside the panes
Wings whir silvery through the chinks
My courtyard faded to an icy
Court of moons with bright red gutters

Made of stars which crystallized this night
Rooms seven I must not wander through
Where planets keep their watch

And with the beam shall they baptize my brow
For which beneath the reign of sleep
He flared abruptly like a folded fan.

[43]

Hat nicht ein Schatten ewigen Bestand
Wenn nur die Sonne ewig scheinen wollte
Daß sie am Himmelszelt hernieder rollte
Macht daß der Schatten in der Nacht verschwand

Doch hat in meiner Nacht ein zweiter Brand
Ein Sonnenball der nicht versinken sollte
Sich aufgehoben und die drinnen grollte
Verzweiflung gab ihm einen Flammenrand

Die neue Sonne ist mein ewiges Denken
Gedanken Strahlen die zur Erde lenken
Und ausgestreut sind im geheimsten Ringe

Das All erscheint in ihrem Licht geringe
Doch wunderbar um Götter draus zu tränken
Bist du der Schatten dieser nichtgen Dinge.

Has not a shadow everlasting Being
Would the sun but shine forever
When with heaven's vault it did wheel down
Then was that shadow lost inside the night

Yet in my night a second blaze
A sphere of sun which should not sink
Has raised itself and the despair curled up
Within did lend to it a rim of flame

The new sun is my endless thinking
My thoughts the rays which veer to earth where they
Are strewn inside a most mysterious ring

The universe appears in their light meager
Though strangely so that gods are watered from it
Thou art the shadow of these empty things.

44

Der noch in gesenkten Götterhänden
Brennt der Stern der dich zum Sterben rief
Zielet mir ins liebste Leben tief
Schnelle Pfeile die mich heil entwenden

Was die wache Seele irr durchlief
Ward schon reiner Schein aus meinen Lenden
Mir entströmt mein Atem ein Verschwenden
Und mein Schatten steht im Abend schief

Weil sich tausend Arme nach ihm strecken
Ach die Seele sucht den schwarzen Sammet
Des Vergangnen flüchtend ganz zu decken

Ja mein Dasein steht im Schlaf entflammet
Alle Träume starren von Gefahren
Und nur du bist traumlos zu gewahren.

It burns still in reposeful hands divine
The star which called thee to thy dying
While deep into my dearest life the rapid
Arrows aim which steal me whole and sound

Whate'er the wakeful Soul ran through pell-mell
Did quickly turn to purest semblance from my loins
My breath streams forth in waste from me
My shadow stands aslant in evening light

And stretching towards it are a thousand arms
Ah the Soul in fleeing seeks to cover all
The soft black velvet of things past

Enflamed indeed my Being in sleep
Each dream grows rigid with the peril
And only thou art dreamless to discern.

45

Meine Seele was suchest du immer den Schönen?
Lange ist er schon tot und die rollende Welt ist
Ihrer Umdrehung gefolgt daß nun keiner den Held mißt
Meine Seele was suchest du immer den Schönen?

Warum erweckst du o Herr mich mit Weinen und Stöhnen?
Ach ich suchte den Schlaf und von Klagen entstellt ist
Meine Verlassenheit der du Verlaßner gesellt bist
Warum erweckst du o Herr mich mit Weinen und Stöhnen?

Also hielt ich eines Nachts Zwiesprach im Herzen
Und verstummte beschämt entschlossen zu schweigen
Meiner Seele nicht mehr meine Trauer zu zeigen

Nicht mir zum Trost sie zu wecken in meinen Schmerzen
Aber siehe sie ließ aus dem schlafenden Munde entsteigen
Trauriger Lieder viel Ihre Tränen entbrannten wie Kerzen.

My Soul why art thou always in search of the Beautiful one?
Long is he dead and the rotating globe so
Attends to its spinning that no one still misses the hero
My Soul why art thou always in search of the Beautiful one?

Why dost wake me O Lord with such weeping and groaning?
Ah I was looking to sleep and lamenting disfigures
My desolate state in which Desolate one thou dost share
Why dost wake me O Lord with such weeping and groaning?

And so one night I held in my heart a debate
Falling mute and ashamed I determined on silence
No longer my sorrow to show to my Soul

No more to wake her my griefs to assuage
Though see from her mouth sleeping she allowed to ascend
So many a sorrowful song Her tears flaring like candles.

46

Es ist der Herrscher Tod der Lust vertauschet
Daß rote Fahne weht in Not gehißt
Vom Boot der Liebe das zu später Frist
Die Stürme stürzen Nacht in Wogen rauschet

Die Sinkenden einwiegt sein Singen wißt
Wie Eure Fahrt vom Tode war belauschet
Ich bin und war der Euer Segel bauschet
Und Finsternis und Licht aus Wolken gießt

Der Euch im reineren Zenithe wies
Den Stern von schwesterlichen Los und Glauben
Die welkenden Gefühlen überdies

Aus Eurem Kranze las und Flug der Tauben
Um Eure Stirne senkt zum Meeresbade
Und salbte Euren schmalen Mund mit Gnade.

Ruler Death does occupy the place of Joy
So flies the red flag hoisted in distress
Upon the boat of Love which storms will
Topple at the time appointed night roars in the waves

His singing lulls to sleep those sinking know Ye
How upon Your voyage Death did spy
I am and was the one who fills Your sails
And from the clouds spills dark and light

He who pointed out to You the star
Of sisterhoodly faith and fate inside a purer zenith
And even more did pluck out wilting feelings

From Your wreath who sinks a flight of doves
About Your brows for their sea-bath
And salved Your narrow mouths with grace.

47

Solange Nacht das Dunkel hält gebreitet
Für Tier und Mensch die schläfert es im Raume
Netzt unser Lager Feuer aus dem Traume
Der in dem Herz der toten Freundin streitet

Vor Dämmer während in dem breiten Baume
Der Vogel ruft der scheu den Tag geleitet
Der Schatten in den langen Gräsern gleitet
Umkränzet Glut das Grab am schwarzen Saume

Der Morgen wendet sich auf dieser Stätte
Zur Nacht zurück die kühle Winde sendet
Der Nachmittag verbirgt im Rasenbette

Sich vor dem Strahle welcher feindlich blendet
Und als es Mittag war hat mit den Stunden
Sich all sein Licht in ihrem Grab gefunden.

So long the night does hold its darkness spread
For beast and man who drowsy grow in space
Our couch shall wetted be by fire from the dream
Which quarrels inside the dead girl's heart

Before the dawn while in the spreading tree
The bird calls out who shyly ushers in the day
And shadow glides amid tall grasses
Flames enwreathe the grave by the black bed

Upon this site the morning does turn back
To night which sends cool winds
The afternoon conceals itself inside the lawn

Before the beam which hostile blinds
And with the midday all his light had found itself
Beside the hours in her grave.

48

Wie stürzt Erinnern aus verlaßnem Tann
Zur Ruh im Lethestrom unstillbar drängend
Die junge Flut durch jähe Schlüfte zwängend
Im engen Tale das ihr Lust entsann

Die Finsternis mit ihrer Gicht besprengend
Da späte Sonne hinterm Fels entrann
Und schweren Schlaf im Nebelmeer gewann
Herz unermeßlich überm Grunde hängend

Doch harret die sich nimmermehr betrübt
An der Vergängnis stetigen Gesetzen
Und die den Abendgang am Strand geübt

Wo blaue Wellen ihre Füße netzen
Aufblickt verweilend aus der steten Bahn
Mit letztem Sinn dem Freunde zugetan.

Out from the lonely stand of pine spills Memory
Implacable her press towards peace in Lethes's stream
Her young flood made to squeeze through drastic gorges
In the straitened vale which did bring joy to mind

Sprinkling darkness with her surge of spray
When the late sun did flee behind a cliff
To win deep slumber in a sea of cloud
Her heart unfathomed hanging o'er the abyss

Yet she who never more shall grieve
Clinging to the constant laws of Pastness
Having had her evening promenade upon the shore

Where azure wavelets damp her feet
Out from the steadfast course looks up lingers
Her last thought given to the friend.

49

Das war ich wußt es wohl die letzte Fahrt
Auf lichten Wellen haschte noch der Wind
Mich schläferte ich fühle nur gelind
Mich an Euch lehnen deren Gegenwart

Mir aufgetan jedoch verwandelt ward
Zum schwarzen Scheine aus erschloßnem Spind
Das ist mein Traum Gestalt gewinnt
Das Kommende Ihr seid in mir verwahrt

Wie Eures Geistes himmlisches Gesind
Entfaltet nach der Spiegelbilder Art
Sich ewiglich einander so gepaart

Wie Dichter sich im eignen Lied besinnt
Muß es geschehen daß Ihr bald erfahrt
Wie Ewigkeit der Lieb gesonnen zart.

It was the final voyage well I knew
The wind still caught at shining waves
I drowsy grew I only feel myself
So mildly lean on You whose presence

Opened wide for me though altered now
A shining blackness from the unlocked panel
That is my dream and what is coming
Finds its shape In me are You kept safe

A heavenly household of Your Spirit
Unfolded as are images inside a mirror
Eternally mated one thus with the other

As in his poem the poet thinks himself to see
Surely shall You soon discover
How tenderly eternity does favor love.

50

Das brennende Gedenken beugte nah
Sich auf den Bram der Zeit um Kühlung neigend
Doch der in seinem Spiegel wiederzeigend
Wies ihn allein und gleiches Leid geschah

So Nacht wie Tag daß gramverzehrt und schweigend
Sehnsucht verblieb die ihn im Fieber sah
Bis tröstend er mit der Gewährung "Ja"
Und der Vergebung stumme Hymne zeigend

Die Bilder all entführte und die Zeichen
Befreiter Blick trat in den Wendekreis
Der hohen Trauer wo sich aus den bleichen

Wintern errichtete das neue Reis
In dessen Kelchen schlummerten die Samen
Kommender Kinder aus gelobtem Namen.

Ardent Remembering did bend near
Inclining toward Time's topsail for its cooling
Which however by reflection in its glass
Showed him alone and night and day

A like pain coming silent Yearning stayed
Consumed with grief to watch him in his fever
Til he yielded and consolingly
Did gesture with his mute forgiving hymn

And make off with all images and signs
His gaze now freed stepped in the tropics
Of high sorrow where fresh growth

Did raise itself out of pale winters
And in whose cups there slumbered seeds
Of coming children from the praiséd Name.

51

Wie karg die Maße der gehäuften Klagen
Wie unerbittlich das Sonett mich bindet
Auf welchem Weg die Seele zu ihm findet
Von alledem will ich ein Gleichnis sagen

Die beiden Strophen die mich abwärts tragen
Sind jener Gang der im Gestein sich windet
In welchem Orpheus' Suchen fast erblindet
Es ist die Lichtung hier des Hades Tagen

Wie dringend er Eurydike erbat
Wie warnend Plutos sie ihm gab anheim
Wird nicht bedeutet von dem kürzern Pfad

Sind Zeugnis die Terzinen doch geheim
Bleibt wie sie unsichtbar ihm Folge tat
Bis sie sein Blick verscheucht der letzte Reim.

How poor the measures for my heaped complaint
How ruthlessly the sonnet limits me
By what path the Soul returns to him
For all these things I shall propose a likeness

The two strophes which bear me downward
Are that path which winds through rock
In which Orpheus's search turns nearly blind
Here now the clearing inside Hades's days

How he urgently did beg Euridice
With what warnings Pluto gave her to him
The shorter passage does not signify

The tercets are a witness and yet hidden still
The way she made to follow him unseen
Until his look drives her away the final rhyme.

52

In aller Schönheit liegt geheime Trauer
Undeutlich nämlich bleibt sie immerdar
Zwiefach und zwiefach unenträtselbar
Sich selbst verhüllt und dunkel dem Beschauer

Sie gleicht nicht Lebenden in ihrer Dauer
Kein Lebender nimmt sie im Letzten wahr
An ihr bleibt Schein wie Tau und Wind im Haar
Je näher nahgerückt je ungenauer

Sie steht wie Helena im Dämmerlicht
Der beiden Welten Sprache taugt ihr nicht
Es sei denn blendend ihr Geflect zu trennen

Doch war es deiner Schönheit nicht gegeben
Als offner Tod aus deinem Jugendleben
Zu wachsen und sich selber zu benennen?

In all Beauty lies a secret sorrow
For obscure she ever shall remain
Twice times two a cipher never to be broken
Veiled unto herself and dark to him who looks upon her

Unlike the living she in her enduring
None who lives discerns her last degree
Semblance clings to her as wind and dew in hair
The closer brought the vaguer seeming

She stands like Helen in the twilight
Words of neither world will suit her
Save her tresses blinding be undone

And yet was not unto thy beauty given
The honest death out of thy Jugendleben
To grow and give itself a Name?

53

Es ist ein Kahn mit solcher Fracht
Wie noch kein Schiff sie jemals trug
Es steht der Name Herz am Bug
Wohin er wohl die Reise macht?

Barre von Gedächtnis sind die Tracht
Darüber Teppiche genug
Gesträhnter Sehnsucht und ein Krug
Von Tränenerz aus Mitternacht

Du siehst auf diesem großen Kahn
Nicht Segel Mast noch Steuermann
Kein anderer kreuzt in den Bereichen

Ihn wirft die Woge hin und her
Von seiner Fahrt verbleibt kein Zeichen
Und seine Fracht verfällt zum Meer.

Here is a barque with such strange freight
As no ship ever yet did bear
The name of Heart stands on its bow
Where might its journey be?

Bars of memory are the cargo
Over which are rugs enough
With strands of yearning and a jug
From midnight with brass tears

And on this barque so grand you see
Nor sail nor mast nor steering man
No other barque will cross these zones

The waves they toss it to and fro
Its passage leaves no sign behind
Its freight falls to the sea.

54

Wie soll ich messen diese Einsamkeit?
Erteilte Schmerz mir noch die alten Stöße
So deckten sie einander ihre Blöße
Der namenlose Rhythmus war ihr Kleid

Nun aber leide ich die nackte Zeit
Mit einem Gang auf dem ich nichts verflöße
Verfährt mein innrer Strom in seiner Größe
Nicht weint das Herz mehr ob der Mund auch schreit

Wann ist ein Neujahr meiner Leiden da
Und wann bin ich der Trauer wieder nah
Nach der ich in ertaubten Tagen darbe

Ach wann erglüht in ihrer schwarzen Farbe
Am Haupt des Jahrs wie ich sie damals sah
Des flammenden Augustes tiefe Narbe?

How should I survey this loneliness?
When pain still dealt me out its former blows
So each would hide the bareness of the last
Their dress a nameless rhythm

Now instead I suffer naked Time
At such a rate that I let nothing flow away
My inner stream but strays within its vastness
My heart no longer weeps though yet my mouth will shout

When comes a New Year's for my suffering
And when shall I be once more close to grief
For which in these numb days I languish

Ah when begin to glow in all its black
Upon the Year's Head as I saw it then
The deep scar of an August gone to flame?

Ich bin ein Maler der aus Schatten
Das wunderbarste Bildnis malt
Und teurer seine Farben zahlt
Als andre ihre vollen satten

Wenn keiner mehr von ihren prahlt
Erglühen noch die meinen matten
Wie über schweren Grabesplatten
Ein altes Mosaik erstrahlt

Und doch steht Nacht vor meinen Augen
Von Tränen deckt sie ein Visier
Sie müssens aus dem Innern saugen

Mit sehnsuchtstrunkener Begier
Dann wird es als ein Urbild taugen
Dir selber ähnlich ähnlich mir.

I am a painter who from shadows
Paints a most astounding likeness
And dearer for him are his colors
Than for others theirs so rich and full

When no one longer boasts of theirs
Still shall my dull tints glow
As old mosaics send forth rays
Above grave markers squat and low

And yet night stands before my eyes
A visor made of tears is over them
Greedy must they suck the thing

From deep inside with drunken wild desire
Then will it fitly make an Urbild
As of thee the likeness as of me.

56

Du hast mein Leben uns vor sieben Jahren
Ein Kind geboren Ohne Schwangerschaft
Entließest du's in engelhafter Kraft
An einem Tag voll Blut und voll Gefahren

Seit diesem Tage hält es uns in Haft
Wenn unsre Lippen allzu heiß sich paaren
Wenn wir in Spiel und Reden unfromm waren
Tritt uns vor Augen Trauer die uns straft

Warum will dieses Kind nicht andern gleichen
Oft flüchtet es vor uns gleich einem Wilde
Und Schweigen und Vergehen führt's im Schilde

Wo andre blühen muß es wachsend bleichen
Und längst entwächst es unseren Bereichen
Und nimmt nur Nahrung an von seinem Bilde.

Seven years ago, my Life, thou didst
Present us with a child And not once pregnant
Wast delivered with angelic power
The day was full of danger full of blood

Since that day it holds us captive
When our lips mate with too much heat
When unclean are we in speech and play
Chastizing sorrow steps before our eyes

Why will this child not be as others
Often it does flee us like a savage and
Against us plot some soundless trespass

Where others bloom it only goes pale growing
And long since growing past our reach
Is nourished only by his image.

57

Wenn du dem Rausch der Irrfahrt dich verwehrst
—Wer singt die Jahre deiner Odyssee
Dein Meer war Mißmut und dein Wind war Weh—
Und wieder Einlaß in dies Haus begehrst

Das du o Schmerz vor allen andern ehrst
Harrt dir auch drinnen weder heut noch je
Nicht Eurykleia nicht Penelope
Wenn du einst dennoch wieder zu mir kehrst

Dann denke ich wie mächtig muß es dröhnen
Beschreitest du die ausgetretnen schönen
Durch diesen alten Leib gelegten Stiegen

Und wieder: wie unhörbar und verschwiegen
Ertastest du nach den vertrauten Plänen
Den Zugang zu der Kammer meiner Tränen.

If thou shouldst save thyself from wander-frenzy
—Of thine odyssey who sings the years
Ill-humor was thine ocean woe thy wind—
And wish to gain admittance to this house once more

Which thou, o Pain, dost honor over all the rest
Within shall be awaiting thee upon that day or any
Neither Eurykleia nor Penelope
Though if thou shouldst sometime return to me e'en so

I wonder then how loud must be the thunder
Shouldst thou mount the worn-out goodly steps
Which laid were by this wasted body

And again: How soundlessly and with what stealth
From plans well known to thee thy touch
Might know its way into the chamber of my tears.

58

Wenn ich ein Lied beginne
So hält es ein
Und werd ich deiner inne
Es ist ein Schein

So wollte dich die Minne
Gering und klein
Auf daß ich dich gewinne
Mit Einsamsein

Drum bist du mir entglitten
Bis ich erfuhr
Nur fehlerlosen Bitten

Verrät Natur
Und nur entrückten Tritten
Die selige Spur.

When I begin a song
It ceases
And should I then perceive thee
Tis a phantom

So Love's courting wished thee
Slight and small
That I should win thee for myself
With mere being alone

Thus thou didst escape me
Til I saw that
Nature heeds

But flawless pleas
And only shows to steps away from earth
The blessed trace.

59

Ich weiß nicht ob die Worte die dir gelten
Und die ich als geheimes Ingesinde
Manchmal im Torweg meiner Lippen finde
Auf Sohlen des Merkur sich zu mich stellten

Ob sie nicht vielmehr aus den innern Welten
Verjährter Fron entlediget geschwinde
Auffuhren für Prophetische und Blinde
Durch Schachte die sich vormals nicht erhellten

Drum weiß ich nicht: bewege ich mit Beten
Die Unerbittlichen zu mir zu treten —
Sie gehn und kommen mit Gelegenheiten

Entbiete ich alle Tage lang mein Rufen
Zu ihnen nieder über Sturz und Stufen
Sie hören nur auf deines Bluts Gezeiten.

I know not if the words describing thee
And which I sometimes find to be
A secret household in the gateway to my lips
Did reach me on the soles of Mercury

Or else their villein service being done
They swiftly rose from inner worlds
For prophecies and for the blind
Through shafts which had not ever shone

And so I do not know: Shall my prayers
Move unpitying words to step to me—
Which go and come as well they please

Or shall my cries be sent to those
Forever down and over cataracts and ledges
Which harken only to the tidal motion of thy blood.

60

Gibst du mir nachts ein Lied an dich ein
Wollt im Erwachen
Ich ihm Worte von denen leihn
Welche wir sprachen

Wenn wir die süßen im Abendschein
Früchtegleich brachen
Weckte in unseren Blicken der Wein
Zögerndes Lachen

Ihrer keines mehr neiget sich je
Und ich erlerne
Nur ein unerschöpfliches Weh

Faßt als Zisterne
Nun im Widerschein der Idee
Früchte und Sterne.

If nights thou shouldst send me a song of thyself
So would in waking
I wish for it words among those
Which we spoke

When in twilight we plucked our sweet speech
Like ripe fruit from the tree
And wine woke in our glances
A hesitant laughter

Such fruit shall no more to us bend
And I only master
An endless unwearying woe

Which like a cistern
Reflecting the Idea
Grasps fruit and stars.

61

Verschwiegener Laut alleiniges Gewand
Das Abgeschiednen unverweslich bleibt
Und unverlierbar Name einverleibt
Sind sie in dich durch ihren neuen Stand

Vollkommne Wehr die keinem sich verschreibt
Den noch ein Schauer an das Leben bannt
Stahlblauer Panzer über dessen Wand
Vegangenes in Spiegelbildern treibt

Es sind mit dir die Schönen angetan
Damit die Seelen nicht vergeblich nahn
Der Trauernden für die dein Widerschein

Die Dinge sterben läßt doch ungemein
Geheimere im Innern leben macht
Erhabner Name starre Totentracht.

O secret Sound the one and only dress
Worn by the dead without decay
Inalienable Name through their new state
Are they made part of thee

The perfect stronghold which shall yield to none
Whom yet one tremor binds to life
A steel-blue shield across whose face
Things past drift images reflected from a glass

Tis with thee the Beautiful are clad
So grieving souls draw near and not in vain
Those for whom thy second shining

Lets plain things die and yet makes live
Within them much more secret ones
Exalted Name stiff costume of the dead.

62

Schlägt nicht die Stunde Herz und steht im Tor
Nicht endlich der um den du lang gerungen
Der große Schmerz der Herr der tausend Zungen
Des Einlaßklage schallt so laut empor

Daß allen Herzens Kammern aufgesprungen
Die er zu seiner Wohnstatt auserkor
Und aus dem Innern im befreiten Chor
Des Freundes Stimme tritt von Leid umschlungen

Der Glocke gleich von Ewigkeit geschlagen
Und gleich dem Kranz der morgenroten Zeiten
Tönst du mein Herz in lichterfüllten Tagen

Und Stille kann dich nimmermehr geleiten
Gefäß nur bist du eines Gottessanges
Und klingend auf den Fährten deines Ganges.

Strikes not the hour Heart and stands not he at last
Within the gate for whom thou hast long striven
Pain of pain, Lord of a thousand tongues
Whose shout for entry echoes up so loud

That all flung wide thy chambers are
Which he did choose to make his dwelling place
And from within forth steps in sorrow wrapped
My friend's voice amid the liberated choir

Like the bell which everlastingness has struck
And like the wreath of crimson-morning times
Thou my Heart dost sound in light-filled days

And stillness can with thee go never more
Thou but the vessel of a god's song
And sounding in the traces of thy motion.

63

So wie ein Fürst die unbesiegte Bahn
Ins fremde Land beschließt mit sicherm Frieden
Hast du das Leben eh du abgeschieden
Mit makelloser Hand dir untertan

Dann nahmst du—unerkannt und doch gemieden—
Von deinen Treuen die dich scheiden sahn
Des schweren Sieges leichte Palme an
Und nicht erschienst du fürder mehr hienieden

Die Heerschar ist zerstoben und vergangen
Das Land verloren was du angefangen
Wer weiß wie lang es unvollendet bleibt

Ich habe mir das Werben und das Bangen
Der höchsten Tage dauernd einverleibt
Und blieb zurück der deine Taten schreibt.

Just as a prince will crown his undefeated way
Into the foreign land with certain peace
So thou with hand unstained didst of Life make
A loyal subject ere thy taking leave

Then didst thou—unacknowledged and yet shunned—
Accept the slender palm of costly victory
From thy faithful ones who saw thee go
And didst no further show thyself among us

Dispersed the troop and melted into air
The land fruitless all by thee begun
Who knows how long it shall remain undone

I have made the wooing and the fearing
Of those highest days a lasting part of me
And stayed behind the writer of thy deeds.

64

Wo sich die Jugend mit dem Tode krönte
Hat sich die Gruft für immer zugetan
Doch legt seitdem der späte Tag dort an
Der herwärts seine letzte Fahrt gewöhnte

Bei seiner Kunst erwacht der große Schwan
Mit hellem Schrei in gelle Frühe tönte
Strömender Mitternächte Leid versöhnte
Als er sich aufhob und auf seiner Bahn

Des Todesschlummers Regenbogen spannte
Von Horizonte zu fernsten Horizonten
Darunter sich im Traum der Schläfer wandte

Erflehend ihn indes die nachtbesonnten
Gefilde ließ und schnelle niederlenkte
Der Schwan zum Hügel den der Tau besprengte.

Where youth did crown itself with death
The vault has sealed itself forever
Yet belated Day e'er since makes landing there
And hither trained his final journey

By his art is roused the great-spanned swan
Whose bright cry when it rose went through the
Shrilling dawn and reconciled the pain
Of streaming midnights and who upon

Its way did bend the rainbow of death's slumber
Horizon to horizon end to very end
And under turned the sleeper in a dream

Imploring it the while it left fields sunning
In the night and veered with haste
Down to the hill made bright with dew.

65

Das Jagen hoch im Blauen will ermatten
Vom Flügelschlage also sinket müd
Der Smetterlinge Paar wo Thymian blüht
Die Seele flog zuvor zum Land der Schatten

Verweilst du hier o mein erstaunt Gemüt
Erinnern sucht im Tod den treuen Gatten
Dies süße Bild ist nimmer zu bestatten
Wo überm Altar noch die Träne glüht

Versagt ist mir dem Blicke zu begegnen
Der überm Morgen wie die Sonne rollt
Die Worte werden nicht mehr niederregnen

Und ihrem Schauer ferne säumt und grollt
Der Seele Anblick die Erinnern flieht
Natur allein im Bilde niederzieht.

To soar the blue aloft will tire
Weary then with thrashing of their wings
The pair of butterflies sink down in blooming thyme
Flown was the Soul unto the shadow land

Dost tarry here O my astounded Heart
In death Remembering seeks the faithful spouse
This sweet image never to be buried
While above the altar tears still burn

No more am I to meet that gaze
Which rolls beyond the morning like the sun
No more shall words come raining down

And for their shower there is slow and distant thunder
To glimpse the Soul which flees Remembering
Nature draws down nothing but an image.

66

O daß ich wieder diesen Ruf vernähme
Von allem was da aufgebaut zu scheiden
Ich wollte seine Stimme nicht vermeiden
Ich ließe alles ginge hin und käme

Vor jene Stimme die da will ich schäme
Mich meiner Zeit und dessen was wir leiden
Wir wurden schmachvoll und gemein bescheiden
Nichts Edles blieb das unsre Not verbräme

Und wie wir suchen und die Nachtheit wenden
Ein Licht in uns zu fangen das uns rette
Enttauchet meinen vorgehalten Händen

Erinnerung der Worte die mich senden
Als deinen Folger auf des Gottes Stätte
Und nichts was außer dem mein Leben hätte.

O that I might hear this call once more
To part from all which is upbuilded here
I would not want to shun his voice but
Leaving all fare thither and so come before

That voice which wants me there I shame
Me of my time and what we tolerate
We grew disgraceful vulgarly demure
No noble thing remained to decorate our lack

And as we search and turn our nakedness
To catch in us a saving light
There rises from my held-out hands

A memory of words which send me
As thy follower to the seat of God
And nothing more my life should have than this.

67

Unendlich arm geworden aller Arten
Von Liebe sind wir Euch allein im Stande
Und unser Leben schwillt schon bis zum Rande
Ebbt noch einmal zurück das ist Erwarten

Noch fiel die letzte nicht der schwarzen harten
In träger Uhr verrinnt der Rest vom Sande
Ihr kennt die Stunde berget im Gewande
Der Einsamkeiten uns die fast erstarrten

Und uns läßt Sesam eingehn die wir harrten
Aus Euren Lebens tief gewissem Pfande
Wir fühlen glühen rosige Standarten

Von Lilien blüht die schützende Girlande
Die Seelen die sich im Gedächtnis wahrten
Bestehn zuletzt allein die hohen zarten.

Grown hugely poor in every kind
Of love now are we fit for You alone
Our life already swelling to the brim
Ebbs back once more and that is Waiting

The last of hours black and bitter did not come
And sand still dwindles in the lazy glass
You know the hour You shelter us in
Lonelinesses we who were grown nearly numb

And "Sesame" admits us waiting ones
On the deep and certain warrant of Your life
We feel the rosy banners start to glow

The shielding garland blooms with lilies
Souls are these who kept themselves in mind
None but the high the tender finally lasting.

68

So reckt sein Tod wie ästiger Korallen
Purpurnen Baum im Meeresschoße loht
Um fürchtige Seele seine Arme rot
Und dem Gewaltigen ist sie verfallen

Mit bitterem Kuß der ihr Verwesung droht
Dem Dienst gelobt sie sich der herben Qualen
Ergebenheit dem herrischen Gefallen
Zum letzten Lohne wählt die letzte Not

Vermessen im verzweifelten Gelage
Bei wüsten Zeiten stiller Lust gedenkend
Den Lethebecher schlürft der trüben Tage

Wie Ewigkeit mit heitern Händen schenkend
Der Seele spendet und das Erbe teilt
Einfalt der Weigernden lebt unverweilt.

So does his death stretch forth red arms a crimson
Tree of branchy corals afire in the bosom of the sea
About the fearful Soul
And she is fallen to the Mighty One

With bitter kiss which threatens her decay
She swears herself in service of harsh tortures
Obedience to the lordly pleasure
For her last reward selects the final misery

And rash in revels of despair
Mid wicked times recalling quiet joy
Sips from Lethe's goblet of gray days

While Eternity with tranquil hand pours out
For her its succor sharing out the legacy
The simpleness of those refusing springs to life.

69

Ihr hieltet Eure Hände nur gewandt
Ins endliche Verstummen ungemein
Habt Ihr gedient um Euer Einsamsein
Aus großer Liebe zu dem letzten Land

So früh am Orte wart Ihr längst allein
Des Geistes Blume nickt Euch zu verwandt
Die Früchte fallen in die leichte Hand
In Eure Wangen schmiegen Winde ein

Der ewge Reigen an der Wolken Wand
Gewahrte nicht Geschwister unterm Rain
Bis heimlich Euch entglitten das Gewand

Aus Euer beider Blöße brach ein Schein
Vor dem der Schleier ihren Sinnen schwand
Und Freundschaft stand im Aug wie Amarant.

Your hands You held but turned
Into the last extraordinary silence
Well earned your solitude
From great love of the final land

So soon arrived long were You yet alone
The flower of the Spirit nods to You as kin
Fruits fall into an easy hand
And curling in Your cheeks are winds

Everlasting dancers on the wall of cloud
Saw not their siblings underneath the ridge
Before Your clothing slyly slipped from You

From Your twofold bareness shining broke
Which caused the veil to vanish for their senses
And in the eye stood friendship like an amaranth.

70

Fortan vor meinem Fuß der Herold geht
Erfüllt mit immer gleichem Ruf die Runde
Die Ewigkeit er singt und singt die Stunde
Wie Orgel süß wie Stürme schneidend weht

Und er tut kund daß jeder Schmerz gesunde
Sich selbt erkennend trete zum Gebet
Daß über jedem Grabe blüht ein Beet
Und daß sich öffne eure alte Wunde

Sein Lied macht wohl die Weite scheu und leer
Die Wolken fliehen fort vor solchem Bläser
Doch folget dem ein unsichtbares Heer

Verwandtes Leid umsteht ihn hoch wie Gräser
Und wendet seine Häupter zu dem Einen
Im Brudergeiste weckt und stillt das Weinen.

Henceforth the herald goes out in front of me
To ever fill the vault with his one shout
He sings Eternity he sings the hour
Like dulcet pipe like lashing storm his breath

And tells to all that every pain shall heal
Itself now knowing shall step up to pray
That over every grave a bed of flowers blooms
And that your wound of old shall open

Could be his song makes shy and void the distant way
Clouds flee before this trumpeter
And yet an unseen host is following him

About whom kindred sorrow high stands like the grass
Bends its heads round to his One
Wakes in brotherhood and stills the crying.

71

Ach alle Morgen die uns je erschrecken
Mit seinem Namen welcher heimberuft
Sind inniger erfüllt als Ambraduft
Es irrt die Seele aus den Nachtverstecken

Empor zu ihm wie zaghaft aus der Gruft
Nach Worten der Verheißung aus den Hecken
Die Hände sich der Auferstehenden strecken
Bläst einst der Himmlische aus reiner Luft

So läßt sein Name unsern Tag beginnen
Bestürzten wie am nahenden Gericht
Wann saget an steht Abend auf den Zinnen

Verkündend Finsternis verlöschend Licht
Und es erhebt auf daß wir ihn ermessen
Unendlichkeit ihr schweigendes Vergessen.

Ah all the morrows that will ever shake us
With that Name of his which calls us home
Are filled more inwardly than scent of amber
Forth strays the Soul from places of night hiding

Lifting towards it as do fearful hands
Of ones about to rise again stretch from the vault
To words of Promise from the hedges
Should ever Heaven's trump blast from pure air

So will his Name allow our day to start
For those struck dumb as with the nearing Judgment
When is heard: Evening stands upon the battlement

Proclaiming darkness putting out the light
And up is raised the cry we measure it
Infinity the keeping silent and forgetting.

72

Also geschah mir diese Nacht im Traum:
Glücklos doch ledig meiner alten Trauer
Erging ich mich im Schwarm ungenauer
Verlarvter Schemem und gewahrte kaum

Wie meinen Schritt behinderte der Saum
Des leichtesten Gewebes dessen blauer
Behang umflorte nahe einer Mauer
Ein Bildwerk das da aufwuchs wie ein Baum

Und wie ein Trümmerstück aus wachen Tagen
Schien jene Form im Traume aufzuragen
Sie schenkte meiner Schwermut das Vertrauen

Das weite Tuch von ihr zurückgeschlagen
Da stand der Leib der blendendsten der Frauen
Und war in schwarzen Marmor ausgehauen.

Tonight this happened to me in a dream:
Luckless and yet freed of my old sorrow
I did make my way inside a swarm of blurry
Shrouded phantoms taking little notice

How my step was hindered by the hem
Of sheerest fabric which hung blue
Close by a wall to veil a sculpture
That was growing upward like a tree

And like a broken fragment out of wakeful days
The form did tower in my dream
It gave my sorrow confidence

To draw the flowing cloth away
Where stood the body of the blindingest of women
And it was carved out of black marble.

73

Vom Weine schütterten die erste Neige
Die Griechen ehe sie zum Mahl sich legten
Dem Gotte hin den sie damit bewegten
Daß Speis und Trank sich ihnen wohl zeige

Wenn ich am Morgen von dem Lager steige
Wo in der langen Nacht die eingehegten
Gefühle und Gedanken sich nicht regten
Bringe ich ein Opfer auch das ich verschweige—

Doch wo die Worte schwesterlich sich ranken
Darf ich es wagen davon auch zu künden:
Von dem Pokal der innigen Gedanken

Wo bis zum Rande sich die Tropfen ründen
Verschütte ich den Überfluß den schwanken
Von meinem Mund an seine Statt zu münden.

Of wine the Greeks before reclining
To their meal poured out first dregs
An honor to the god whom they would move
That meat and drink prove nourishing to them

When I rise mornings from the couch
Where penned-up thought and feeling
Failed to stir the long night through I also
Bring a gift of which I would not speak —

Though where words like sisters clamber up
So may I dare to give some notice too:
Out of the drinking cup of inward thought

Wherein the drops well to the brim
I spill the excess of those lightly clinging
From my mouth to kiss his grave.

Detail from the baptismal font in the cathedral, Freiburg im Breisgau.

COMMENTARY

[01]   This sonnet is the only one among all those Benjamin addressed to Fritz
Heinle to employ the standard Shakespearian number of rhymes — seven — though
these are still disposed according to the Petrarchan pattern (two quatrains followed
by two tercets). Such conspicuous placement, here at the front of his collection,
must represent an homage. Whether Benjamin was signaling his appreciation of
the form of Shakespeare's sonnets, or more his appreciation of the fact that most of
them are addressed to a youth, cannot be known.

Whatever their scheme, very many of Benjamin's Heinle sonnets conclude in
the Shakespearian manner, with a finely pointed rhyming couplet. In Sonnet 1 the
poet gives a final rhymed consent to the images and memories of his friend being
taken from him if only the friend will leave his "sacred Name" to him as an "Amen
without end." Such names are higher and more nearly transcendent than anything
preserved as mere images. (For other "name-sonnets" see nos. 50, 61, and 71.)

Benjamin had been led by his friend Gershom Scholem to a deeper consid-
eration of Jewish mysticism. It is possible that Benjamin's notion of his friend's
"sacred Name" draws from the ideas of the 13th-century kabbalist Abraham Abu-
lafia, who wrote of meditational practices intended to unite the human with the
divine mind; these call for the recitation of divine names while maintaining certain
postures and breathing patterns and for imagining the letters of these names in
succession. Here Benjamin may be proposing to meditate upon the "sacred Name"
of his deceased friend, Fritz Heinle, in a similar way. This Name would not be his
friend's ordinary name but some other, hidden one.

L.4 Literally: "Loose themselves from the lukewarm [tepid] marriage of
things."

L.7 *überbrannt* — Literally, "overburned." A newly invented word which
serves the poet as a bridge between the physicality of his friend's (eloquent) red lips

and the figurative eloquence of his fevered brow: The friend's lips are, as it were, "overburned" by his brow. Here, in translation, these become "burning" and "more burning," respectively.

L.8 *der schwarzen Glimme des Haares* "the black gleam of thy hair" — A photograph purporting to be of Fritz Heinle shows a fair young man (perhaps a "dirty blond," see cover image).

L.9–14 *Abbild/Sinnbild/bildlos* "image"/"symbol" /"without image"— Three different words based on the word *Bild* ("picture," "image," "emblem," "symbol"). This root-relationship cannot be reproduced in English.

L.11 *herzoglich* "princely" — Literally, "ducally."

L.13–14 *deinen heiligen Namen ... wie unendlich Amen* "thy sacred Name ... Amen without end"—It is worth noting that in German (as in English) *Amen* and *Name* employ the same four letters; they are anagrams of each other.

[02]

L.3–4 *Kehrte ... in ewige Vergessenheit* "Would turn ... to blankness without end" — Literally, "would turn into eternal oblivion."

L.7 *färbte* "[should] discolor" — Literally, "[should] dye" or "[should] color." Here the verb could also be rendered in English as "discolored," that is, as being in the simple past, which accords with the tense of the verb in the following line (überzog).

L.8 Literally: "Night covered [over] the sea on her light boat."

L.9–10 The poet's sorrow cannot be named in ordinary language and hence is "nameless." It finds an adequate correlate only in remote and silent stars. Benjamin would come to conceive of the heavenly constellations as a special source of revelation — as figures or emissaries of the hidden supersensory world. He was impressed by the belief of the primitive animist that stars, being conscious, gaze down at us as we gaze up at them. Here we may even imagine his friend's "gaze" fixing the poet from above while he gazes at the stars to glean otherwise hidden knowledge of the friend now in Heaven.

L.11 *mit dichter Mauer* "with fortress wall" — Literally, "with a thick wall."

L.13 *Jahrzeit* "season" — Benjamin's coinage, and a touching allusion to the annual Jewish ceremony which commemorates the death of a parent or another member of the family. Yahrzeit, the Yiddish word for this ceremony, is a cognate of the standard German *Jahreszeit* ("season"). Benjamin, marrying German and Yiddish, achieves a linguistically mediated union with his deceased Christian friend.

L.13 *im stillen Stand der Sterne* "In the still patterning of stars" (lines 13–14) — These words anticipate a key phrase of Benjamin's — "the dialectical standstill" (German, *Stillstand*) — that would appear in his later meditations on historical processes and on the possibility of redeeming the past. Other Heinle sonnets in which stillness or silence are a significant motif include nos. 5, 10, 15, 18, 25, and 71.

[03]

L.1 *Du selige Geburt* "Thou blessed Birth" — This birth, familiarly addressed by the poet, is at first difficult to assign.

L.2 *Entstieg ich ihm* "I arose from him" — That is, from the now deceased friend, Fritz Heinle, never to be named in these sonnets. The poet seems to claim to have been born from his friend (who was nearly two years younger); the birth must be a spiritual one.

L.4 Literally: "For the quietest [of those] upon the wide stairs [staircases, steep paths] of Heaven."

L.6 *An welchem* "on which" — Not "in which"; see line 14 and comment.

L.7 *inniger* "more inwardly" — The German, a word of many shades, can mean: "more intimately, "more closely," "more fervently," "more tenderly," "more profoundly."

L.11–12 *Mein Haupt ... die Wiege* "My head ... his cradle" — The image is perhaps borrowed from paintings by Mantegna and other Italian Renaissance artists in which cherubim are shown as winged baby-heads in glowing colors circling the divine mother and child.

L.14 *Führt auf seiner Hand* "leads upon his hand" — An odd usage best translated literally. The audacious imagery of this sonnet evokes a series of physical intimacies between the poet and his friend so as to blur or even efface their separate existences. And even the separation brought about by death produces fresh intimacy: We learn that the poet, too, has suffered a "young death" which has been taken and perhaps led away in the hand of the deceased friend, or rather, "upon his hand." Not the poet's birth only but his death, too, is made to depend upon the friend's.

[04]

L.1 *im Erwachen* "Waking" — It is not clear whose waking is meant, the poet's or his friend's.

L.2 *Fährten* "traces" — A term used by hunters; Fährten are tracks or traces left by the hooves of animals.

L.3 *Und seiner Augen Sternen* "and the starlight of his eyes" — Literally, "and the stars of his eyes." *Augenstern* is the German word for the pupil of the eye and serves figuratively as an endearment, as in "you are the apple of my eye."

L.4 *die . . . stummen Spiegel allen Geistes* "mute . . . the mirrors of all Spirit" — The word *Geist* occurs some ten times in the Heinle sonnets. It is a word notoriously difficult to render in English, since it can mean "mind," "spirit," or "ghost." Moreover, it is a central term in the philosophy of German idealism (Hegel) and therefore is rarely without its philosophical aura. In his sonnets Benjamin sometimes attributes "Geist" to specific persons; or it is treated as a personification. But sometimes it seems to be a more general phenomenon which only visits individual consciousness: The friend's eyes, which do not literally speak, reflect "all Spirit."

L.9 *standen sie wie Lachen* "they stood as pools" — Only two end-rhymes are employed in the sonnet ("-achen" and "-ärten"). *Lachen* ("pools") at the end of line 9 means something entirely different from what the same word had meant two lines earlier at the end of line 7 ("laughter").

L.12–13 *sprachen die Dinge denen Namen noch gebrachen* "would those things speak which yet lacked names" — A cryptic reflection of Benjamin's thinking about the higher stages of language which preceded ordinary human language — stages which he believed originated with God and then were bequeathed to Adam and Eve, and which are to be restored in the messianic time to come. Here his friend's tears contain things which "speak" without help from our postlapsarian language and its names for things. (See also Sonnet 24.)

[05]   Several other sonnets imply hectoring on the part of the poet's friend, or a bitter tone of voice (see the note to Sonnet 8, line 7). Here his friend's voice, seemingly disembodied — and no longer physically audible — has ascended to a heavenly realm where it "streams forth its joy" with God's blessing. For Benjamin, stillness and silence are characteristic of the divine, which remains withdrawn and perhaps entirely beyond our ken.

     L.1 *Du nie mehr klingende* "Thou soundless now forever" — Literally, "Thou never sounding more."

     L.5 *O Stimme* "O Voice" — Four lines must pass before the reader learns the identity of the being who has been familiarly addressed from the outset — namely, the personified voice of the poet's deceased friend. This is a striking instance of "rough [hard] facture" (see Essay Notes, no. 35).

     L.10 *der Geliebten* "the Loved One" — Feminine, to be identified with the deceased friend's voice. In this sonnet there is play back and forth between addressing that voice directly as "thou" or "thee," and indirectly using the feminine third person — the latter a distancing effect not readily achievable in English, which lacks the superb resources of indirection found in German with its three genders for nouns as well as for pronouns and substantive adjectives.

     L.12 *jugendlich* "youthfully" — "Youth" (*Jugend*) was a pivotal term in Walter Benjamin's thinking during his first adult years and supplies the central category for his earliest metaphysical writings. Even so the word does not occur (in any form) otherwise in those fifty sonnets for Heinle which Benjamin chose for publication, and only twice in the remaining twenty-three sonnets (in nos. 52 and 64). On the other hand, "young" (*jung*) occurs five times (see nos. 3, 22, 26, 33, and 48).

     L.14 *den Leib der Stummen* "the body of the Silent One" — Another reference to the friend's voice. Literally, "the body of the Silent [feminine] One."

[06]
     L.4 *aus dem leisem Mund der Toren* "From the murmuring mouth of fools" — Literally, "from the gentle [softly sounding, quiet] mouth of fools." The occurrence of the plural "der Toren" ("of fools") seems odd; one rather expects the singular "des Tors" ("of the fool") with reference to the poet. Here perhaps is an instance of ruthless rhyming at the expense of meaning.

L.8 *Dein Wehen* "thy birth pangs" — Can also be read as "thy waving [fluttering]."

L.9–14 Time-relations in this sonnet are complicated: The poet weeps to think how his friend, dead now, is listening to his rhymes and lending him inspiration, for commemorative verses, from those eloquent songs the friend would sing when still living.

L.14 *ins schwarze Haar* "into thy raven hair" — Once again, as in Sonnet 1, the poet seems to be associating black hair with his friend. "Within his raven hair," with the God of the dead weaving a leafless wreath for his own hair, makes a less likely reading.

[07]   Readers will notice that in this sonnet the poet attributes intellectual leadership to his friend or at the very least, depicts himself as under the sway of the other's thinking (see also sonnets 1, 17, and 21).

L.7 *Zeichen* "runes" — Literally, "signs," "signals," or "marks." A peculiar erotic intimacy results when the friend's *physical* finger etches signs on (or in) the *mind* of the poet.

L.14 *Rätselvollen* "unrevealing" — Literally, "enigmatic" or "puzzling." The bereft poet compares intensely blue sky to eye color and intimates that the eyes of his friend shone with a distant light.

[08]   Sonnet 8 is the first of the truly elusive Heinle sonnets; all in all it suggests comprehensive intimacy between the poet and his friend, with the latter offering the light of his protection to the former. Early on, an intriguing two-foldness in the friend's spirit (*Geist*) is hinted at. This spirit arose as the friend's mother suffered in giving birth to him (line 3) and is somehow associated with blackness (line 6); it made the friend's voice bitter and even brought the poet to tears (lines 7–8). The tercets of the sonnet are especially convoluted: It seems that the poet's "loving" — chiseled as it were phallically into the friend's body (lines 9–10) — engenders "ensouled" beings who are born to the friend and now stand before him as his injured children (lines 11–12). But then the poet implies that he has himself suffered wounds — wounds which are being healed by the friend even after he, the friend, has died.

L.1–2 Literally: "See my life made bright in thy protection which [was] ready to grant [this] out of love ... "

L.5 *in sommerlichen Ähren* "in wheaten summer ears" — Literally, "in summer ears [of corn, wheat]."

L.6 *seines Hauptes* "of his head" — A puzzling turn: The Spirit's head seems to belong to the poet's friend, who is now referred to in the third person. Possibly the sense of the line is: His friend's *Geist* [spirit] makes things like the tassels of corn or ears of wheat turn black which would have stayed blond or fair otherwise.

L.7 *des bittre Stimme* "whose bitter voice"— Another reference to the friend's bitter voice (see Sonnet 1; see also Sonnet 6, line 12, with its mention of the friend's "bitter strophes," and nos. 22 and 57).

L.11 *Die vor dir stehen Kind* "Which stand before thee as a child" — The grammar of this phrase is difficult to rationalize. Some would have the poet address his friend here as "child" (i.e., "which, child, stand before you"). Elsewhere in these sonnets, however, the friend is only ever addressed with "du."

L.13 *ist ... gewesen* "has been" — It may be that Benjamin employs "has been" for rhyming purposes. In any case, one would expect a verb in the second-person singular, in agreement with "[thou] thyself."

[09]   This sonnet as a whole presents a series of baffling images which may harbor glimpses of the Great War with its trenches, exploding shells, and machine-gun fire. Especially mysterious are the beings addressed in lines 2, 4, and 10 with "You" and "Your": Perhaps they are angels who oversee the battlefield, communing with the dead and comforting the living. In other sonnets from this series, the second-person plural clearly points to Benjamin's deceased friend and his friend's lover, and so they may be present here, too. The final line seems to promise a heavenly or spiritual "closer land" liberated directly from the "morning red" of war and death.

Allusions to war or to events related to the outbreak of war in August 1914 are also found in sonnets 11, 15, 22, 28, 54, and 63.

L.2 *Das Euch verweilt zu* "which lingers for Your" — Literally, "which lingers for You as [Your]." Capitalizing second-person plural pronouns is a way to signal respect or reverence; see also sonnets 22, 28, 46, 49, 67, and 69.

L.3 *die Gestalt* "the Form" — A rich word in German. "Form" can be inanimate, i.e., a shape or a pattern, or animate, i.e., a figure, likely a human one. Here, taken in conjunction with "Night" (line 1), *Gestalt* plausibly belongs to those beings referred to in the second person plural, i.e., the sense becomes: "[Your] Form [Figure]." The Figure of these beings would be capable of destroying a sinister (sightless, "blind") spell if only Night were to take leave (see Sonnet 14, note to line 1, and also Sonnet 28, line 7, "blind midnight"). In sonnet 42, "the Figure" will refer to the image of the dead friend.

L.4 Literally: "For You [it] points to the greetings of the dear departed [the dead]."

L.8 *Unsterblichkeit ums Haupt Gewölke ballt* — Can also be construed as: "Clouds do cluster immortality about the head."

L.10 *Helden...die sich süß verschwärmten* "heroes sweetly scattered in their swarming" — *Verschwärmen* as a reflexive verb refers to the scattering of swarms of bees; figuratively, with reference to humans, it can function as an intensifier of *schwärmen* and so mean: "to lose oneself in fantasy" or "to be exceedingly enthusiastic [about someone or something]." Benjamin employs the word reflexively but without a prepositional complement, making one think back to the original sense having to do with bees. An alternative translation would be: "heroes who lost themselves in sweet fantasies."

L.12 Literally: "Darkness for the careworn persons [intently] listening."

[10]

L.4 *Die nahe Schwelle* "The nearby threshold"—Benjamin liked to imagine unseen thresholds separating different planes of existence—for example past, present, and future, mortal and immortal life, or even zones of cities under the sway of differing metaphysical influences. See also sonnets 14 and 29.

L.13 *Mich suchst du nicht* "Me thou shalt not seek" — The sonnet began confidently, with the poet seemingly assured of visits from his deceased friend, but now he declares that the friend will not seek him out.

L.14 *Vor deinen Schein vergangen...mein Scheinen* "Before thy shining... my seeming vanished"—*Schein* and *Scheinen* became terms with special meaning for Benjamin. They feature importantly in his essay *Goethe's 'Elective Affinities'* and in his Habilitationsschrift, *The Origin of the German Mourning Play*. Without a substantial context, the rendering of these words into English remains uncertain. Yet clearly they belong to a semantic spectrum which has for opposing poles the sense of emitting light, or truth ("shining"), and the idea of presenting (mere) appearance ("seeming"). Seeming — through which we first apprehend beauty — can point in the direction of shining. In his Prologue to *The Origin of the German Mourning Play* Benjamin would write: "In this sense he [Plato] declares Truth to be the content of Beauty ... which, however, does not appear by being exposed; rather, it is revealed in a process which might be described metaphorically as the burning up of the husk as it enters the realm of ideas ... "; *vergehen* has many other meanings: "to pass away," "to dwindle [or disappear]," "to pine," "to fade," "to die," "to trespass [or transgress]."

Elsewhere, in other writings, Benjamin develops a concept of ultimate divine reality as "expressionless" and fundamentally inaccessible — as something which humans have almost no chance of nearing on their own and which may never deign to address them. Sonnet 10 represents the transcendent condition of the friend as one of utter stillness and lack of desire, in which there is but "one pulse," and into which space and its dimensions ("South and North") disappear ("melt"). In his letter of November 17, 1913, to Carla Seligson, Benjamin had spoken cryptically of "the fulfillment" which "is too much at rest and too divine to issue from something other than the burning wind."

Lastly: the beginning of line 14 means more than it says. When used accusatively, the preposition *vor* implies a change of place; "vor deinen Schein" therefore suggests something like: "[having come] before thy shining."

[11]   This is the first of several Heinle sonnets which read rather like dream protocols, in which one thing succeeds another seemingly without logical underpinning. Here vague settings shift and three different persons are mentioned; their roles remain mysterious. It seems that one male figure, having prowled about a "white town," is granted sleep and then removed from the earth by angels (lines 6–10). Another male figure, trapped on a battlefield, is shrouded in linen cloth

sent down to him from a woman who is said to share a snowy mountain retreat with the first man (lines 10–14). The sonnet employs a nearly breathless run-on syntax, with an accumulation of enjambments.

Other Heinle sonnets showing a dream-character include nos. 21, 42, 49, and 72.

L.10 *der Freundin Atem* "his lady's breath" —Literally, "breath of the [female] friend. The first unmistakable reference in these sonnets to a female friend or lover appears in connection with a courtly or fairy-tale image which has her lowering down her garments.

L.11–12 *schimmender Granaten Gebüsch* "a bush of gleaming bomb-shells" — The German phrase plays on the derivation of *Granaten* ("grenades") from *Apfelgranaten* ("pomegranates") such that we may almost see the youth protected by an overhanging bush with its shower of shining fruits.

[12]   Benjamin is known to have read Ernst Bloch's *Geist der Utopie* [The Spirit of Utopia], 1919, with great interest; in this book, music is considered to be uniquely capable of adumbrating messianic time. Song — or Benjamin's idea of it — governs Sonnet 12 from beginning to end. Here remembering and forgetting the deceased friend are to cancel each other in song which ascends from the differentiae of ordinary experience into timelessness. To sustain a lyric mood, Benjamin turns to "smooth facture," with line-oriented syntax and unforced end-rhymes, the lulling interrupted only by a jarring last line.

Other Heinle sonnets in which memory, remembering, or forgetting are prominently featured include nos. 13, 14, 15, 27, 48, 50, 55, and 71.

L.6 *Winden* "weeds" — Specifically denotes "bindweed."

L.14 *ging* "went" — An unprepared shift to the simple past tense abruptly challenges the timelessness evoked until now and reminds us of the death of the poet's friend.

[13]   This sonnet may hint at feelings of unease or guilt on the part of Benjamin towards his friend — to which the first line ("Too late our weary watch did wake") gives preliminary expression. Both "Prayer" (line 5) and "pleading memories" (line 12) would then belong to the poet. "The scales of judgment"

(line 11) bend in favor of the deceased friend and fail to assuage the guilt of the poet, whose memories invade the dead friend's dream "which shall never quiet them" (lines 13–14). The idea that dream contents, or dreams themselves, come from outside the dreamer reoccurs in Benjamin's *Berlin Childhood* ("A ghost") as well as in his *Berlin Chronicle* (see especially notice 21).

A suggestion of unease or guilt on the part of the poet will make itself felt anew in Sonnet 39.

L.5 *So muß sich Andacht* "And so must Prayer" — "Prayer" behaves like a figure in some allegory who is set in motion (along with Death). From here to the end of the sonnet there is no interruption, no stemming of motion; the undulating lines ride on renewed enjambments.

L.9 *sein Wort* "his words" — The masculine pronouns which populate the tercets of the sonnet refer to the poet's dead friend, already alluded to in lines 3–4 ("the sinking of that brow . . . our doubtful trust").

L.10–11 *sieht . . . er* "he sees" (line 10) — Noteworthy is the way the verb *sieht* so far anticipates its subject, *er*. Translation cannot reproduce the striking "rough facture" of the tercets of this sonnet.

[14]   As in Sonnet 10, light supplies the culminating motif here. The poet is at one with the night (lines 1–2) and has suffered an eclipse (line 7) but he is sent a special light which belongs only to the night and will illuminate other worlds for him. This light, issuing from the moon, comes to him as Memory and allows him to commune with his dead friend.

Altogether one finds references to light in more than one-third of the Heinle sonnets — to light contrasted with the dark or with the night, to starlight, moonlight, twilight, sunlight, to light in the eyes of the poet's friend (sonnets 3, 4, 7, and 19). Inevitably, this is spiritual light finding its reflection in one or another aspect of the natural world. Then, too, Benjamin attributes the quality of "shining" to a considerable variety of persons and things and mentions an assortment of heavenly bodies and events. Finally, a "beam" makes its appearance at several critical moments. Sonnets which feature light or shining prominently include (besides nos. 10 and 14) nos. 19, 21, 23, 32, 37, 43, 47, 49, and 69.

L.1 *im Bunde mit der alten Nacht* "in league with ancient Night" — References to the night, or to Night, occur in these sonnets almost as frequently as do those to light or shining, and the approach of night is hinted at in still others. Relations here between darkness and light are complex, even paradoxical (see Sonnet 37, final note). At times the word seems to invoke the general darkness of the war which was dragging on as Benjamin was writing his sonnets (see especially Sonnet 28 and the comment for no. 21, lines 7–8).

L.5 *zu Einer macht* "making … into One" — See Sonnet 39, notes for lines 6 and 9.

L.7 *mein Verfinstern* "that eclipse of me" — By dying, the poet's friend caused him to go into eclipse; *gemieden* "shunned" — Can also mean "avoided."

L.10 *Sie* "She" — The night personified.

L.13–14 *Kein andres Licht … Erinnerung sein Mond* "No other light … Memory his moon" — In *Berlin Childhood* Benjamin will once again associate light with memory (see "Winter evening") and will meditate upon the otherworldliness of that moonlight which allows him to sense a second existence (see "The moon").

L.14 *Geselle* "bedfellow" — Literally, "companion [comrade, mate]."

[15]   Sonnet 15 contributes another facet to the Benjaminian motif of stillness. From it, we gather that the death of his friend has caused ineffable calm to take over the poet's life; some previously active vital principle is suspended in him. The present sonnet is also the first of a goodly number to employ the figure of a ship or of sailing (see also nos. 17, 21, 46, 49, and 53).

L.4 *Segelwald* "flock of sails" — Literally, "forest of sails."

L.7 Literally: "The broad surface [of the sea] grew unnamably [ineffably] calm."

L.11 *Blust* "water-bloom" — Literally, a "bloom" or "blooming" (with no watery connotation).

L.12 *Garben* "sheaves" — Possesses the secondary meaning of "bursts of fire," as from a machine gun.

L.14 *des blendenden August* "of deceiving August" — World War I began and Fritz Heinle took his own life in the first days of August 1914. The first meaning of *blenden* is "to blind"; the word can also mean "to dazzle the sight, to

220

blind through brightness," and by extension, "to blind to the truth," i.e., to deceive or delude.

[16]   The motif of waiting is an important one in many of Benjamin's writings, and sometimes assumes the proportions of messianic hope. Here the poet is waiting for his pangs of grief to abate. He beseeches his friend, who was himself a poet, to temper these verses and he imagines the friend to be like the mother who stills her child's crying, removes his pains, and rocks him to sleep in her arms.

This sonnet is cast in an irregular (though increasingly insistent) dactylic meter; it has been translated into an irregular iambic meter. Something of a Rilkean note is heard, especially in the quatrains.

See sonnets 30, 33, 35, 54, 57, 62, and 67 for other appearances of the waiting motif.

L.1 Literally: "Those which lament thee, to the verses [lines] of longing and pain."

L.2 *des Geistes erwarten* "a waiting for the Spirit" — One of the goals of the youth culture movement as formulated by its leader, Gustav Wyneken, was for youth to "serve the [Hegelian] Spirit" ("dem Geist dienen"). Benjamin feared this notion would lead to the instrumentalization of *Geist*; in his view, one could only wait patiently for Spirit to manifest itself on its own terms and in its own way.

L.8 *zum Teppich* "for . . . a cover"—The word *Teppich* is used for a variety of protective domestic coverings — rugs and carpets, also wall hangings and tapestries.

L.14 Literally: "Taking to thee [receiving] findings that are consuming [harrowing] for the Soul." Also possible is the reading: "Taking to thee findings of the Soul which are consuming [which would consume me]."

[17]

L.6–8 *Gedenkst du noch . . . deine Stirn berührt* "Dost remember still . . . off the shore" — These lines illustrate Benjamin's way with mutating compound metaphors. Here conversation becomes a sailing ship which then turns into the friend's brow while continuing to behave like a ship.

L.6 *Galeeren* "galleys" — The German word has only a nautical meaning.

L.7 *Schären* "stony islets off the shore"—The term for small islands which resulted when continental ice sheets withdrew, scouring and shearing away the surface of the land; they are especially characteristic of coastal waters off Scandinavia and Canada and often occur in clusters.

L.14 *Harfen* "harps" (line 13)—The plural form must have been chosen, despite its very odd effect, to complete the rhyme scheme of the sonnet.

[18]

L.3 *mit des Schweigens Immergrün* "with the evergreen of silence"—Permanent silence should provide a halo for the friend's singing now that his earthly song has ceased.

L.6 *der gebenedeiten Wunden* "for dearly blessed wounds"—A phrase traditionally used to refer to the wounds Christ received during his crucifixion.

L.8 *wie Fanfaren sprühn* "like fanfares fly"—The German evokes an image of flying sparks.

L.12 *Weht atmend* "And breathe warm breath"—Literally, "[My mouth] breathing blows." In breathing on his friend to prevent winter from covering him the poet seeks, metaphorically, to preserve the memories of him.

L.13 *Dies alles tat er mir* "All this he did for me"—Also carries the more immediate sense of: "All this he did to me."

L.14 *gelöst den Riem* "and all undone"—*Riem* (or Riemen) means "[leather] strap," "thong," or "lace." "Gelöst den Riem" translates literally as "[having] loosed [freed] the lace." Death must be the unnamed party responsible.

[19]

L.2 *In seinem Namen* "In his name"—The reference ("his") does not go back to the Spirit (line 1) but refers forward to a never identified person who assumes a presence-in-absence in the course of the sonnet (references to "hands," line 5, to "eyes," line 8, and to "the fugitive," line 14).

L.4 *Venus gibt Bescheid* "Venus gives her order"—Literally, "Venus hands down her decision."

L.6 *tauchet aus den Händen sonder Mühen* "emerge unlabored from the hands" — Literally, "emerge without straining from the hands." Possibly the hands are lifeless and can offer no resistance to the emerging sky.

L.7 *verfrühter* "untimely" — In the sense of "premature"; *der jüngsten Zeit* "from time's end" — That is, when ordinary human time shall be at an end and eternity begins.

L.10 *um die Dächer ... kragt* "stands about the roofs" — Benjamin employs an odd verb, found in neither Grimm nor in Duden, related to the ordinary German for "collar" (*Kragen*). Perhaps one should picture a silhouette of roofs surrounded by a "collar" of blinding bright morning light. (*Auskragen* is an architectural term for a projecting course, or corbeling.)

L.12 West "Zephyrus" — The gentle west wind; the god Zephyrus in Greek mythology.

L.14 *Den Flüchtenden verfolgt ... versunken* "Pursue the fugitive ... sunk from view" — The west wind will pursue the dead friend who has already rounded the horizon — his movement akin to the motion of a heavenly body traveling in the wrong direction: As the physical sun rises in the east, "the fugitive" sinks out of sight, also in the east. The sonnet as a whole associates an elusive, mystical anti-natural light with the poet's friend and his afterlife.

[20]   The first of many Heinle sonnets to insinuate that the poet's friend was a Christ-like figure. Various of them imply that the friend left behind disciples, that he suffered for the sake of the world, or that he left the world and ascended to some heavenly place. See also sonnets 22, 29, 30, 31, 39, 41, 63, and 66.

L.1 *Vergängnis* "Pastness" — A rare word, so rare as to elude firm definition, not to be found in standard dictionaries (Duden, Grimm) and only sporadically online. This word appears also in a rubric which Benjamin noted while planning the scheme for his sequence of fifty sonnets. There "Vergängnis und Gedenken" ("Pastness and Commemoration") appears as the topic for nos. 19–23. The same word is also employed in Sonnet 48. Perhaps for Benjamin *Vergängnis* is surrounded by the aura of *Verhängnis* ("fate").

L.3 *die Geige* "the bow" — Literally, "the fiddle."

L.4 *Wälderhallen* "sounding woodland halls" — Literally, "forest [woodland] halls." The German word cunningly suggests echoing (as a verb *hallen* means to "sound" or to "resound").

L.5 *zur Einkehr aller Wesen lädt* "it invites the turning in of all" — Can also mean: "invites all creatures to a turning inward [in order to meditate]."

L.6 *Sein Tod* "his death" — A reference to the poet's deceased friend, who may already be present with the dancer of the first quatrain.

L.9 *Das Szepter Seliger* "A scepter of the blessed" — That is, a scepter for the deceased who are enjoying a blessed afterlife.

L.10 *Zeitlichkeit* "time passing" — Literally, "temporality": ordinary, eroding time as we experience it.

L.14 *Weil der verlacht* "For whom . . . mocked." — These words call to mind Jesus Christ.

[21]   The sonnet traces an obscure struggle for the poet's (personified, feminine) Soul, over which his friend continues to exert great power even as she is presenting herself "before the Lord" (line 10). The events recorded here seem to belong to a dream from which the Soul wakes suddenly, as from the source of her light and life.

L.1–2 *Als mich die Stimme rief . . . ward ich . . . entrissen* "Summoned by that voice . . . I was . . . dragged" — Once again, and now from beyond the grave, the poet feels himself overcome by his friend.

L.5 *Von ihm der kommt im Wind . . . mit Wissen* "From him who comes in wind . . . with knowing" — Certain attributes of the friend, sources of his power, are named even as he is not.

L.7–8 The friend is filled with light; though whether the light is visible is uncertain, for *birgt* can mean "hides" as well (See also Sonnet 23, line 10).

Benjamin's suggestive letter to Herbert Blumenthal (Belmore) from the year 1916 (see Essay Notes, no. 19) alludes to the war as overall darkness, as Night, which must be made to yield its inner light. Here it is the friend who "stores sheer light in his breast lent him out of darknesses." Perhaps the evils of war are those "darknesses" providing the friend his "sheer light."

L.12 *um ihn* "for sake of him" — The reference is not clear, but seems to be to the friend, who has been drawing the poet and his Soul onward, and not to God.

L.13 *aus ihm der ihren Tag gebiert* "from him who did give birth unto her day" — A second unclear reference, also apparently to the friend.

[22]   The poet vows never to cease mourning his friend — who even in life was a source of pain to him (line 8; see also sonnets 1, 6, 8, and 57). In a rhetorical turn, he lists several conditions, which, if met, might appease his grief (lines 9–12). But these are not likely to be met. With his mention of the "easy effort" of his friend's dying hour, i.e., his suicide, the poet hints for the first time that Fritz Heinle's moral clarity made his choice to die an easy one. (See also sonnets 28 and 52, and for what seems a contrasting view, no. 68).

L.1 *Ihr meine Lippen wollt Euch* "Wish You my lips" — Here Benjamin in his MS has capitalized a second-person plural pronoun which does not refer to Fritz Heinle and Rika Seligson.

L.2 *Und ungeheilt verharschen* "to seal yourselves unhealed" — *Verharschen* refers to the closing up of wounds by means of scabbing.

L.6 *der dem Freund eigen* "which is my friend's" — The poet's voice is dedicated to mourning the death of his friend.

L.7 *heillos* "hopeless" — The German word is applied to dreadful things or situations which cannot be remedied.

L.12 Literally: "[Not before] the world-morn reddens because it is bleeding from it [the friend's "dying hour," line 11]"; the word *Weltmorgen* ("world-morn") is rare and may refer here to the outbreak of the Great War, a morning of world import.

L.14 *des Aufgangs Spiegelbild* "the mirror of his rising" — The image is of a heavenly body as it first rises over the horizon and is reflected in a calm sea. Attributing this rising into the sky to the poet's friend remains an artifact of translation.

[23]
L.4 *Sah ich das Feuer* "I saw the fire" — The image of fire runs through nearly the whole of the sonnet. Here, as in several previous sonnets (nos. 10, 21), the poet's friend is imagined to harbor light.

L.11 *Das Weltall unter seinen Brauen* "The universe beneath his brows" — Another reading, less plausible, would be: "The universe beneath its brows," with "its" referring to "a fire" (line 10).

L.13 *Geblendet* "Dazzled" — With the sense of being led astray or being deceived by an object of fascination.

L.14 *Sein Leben das mir zugemessen* "His life which was assigned to me" — The final line of this terse sonnet in iambic tetrameter makes an unmistakable reference to the friend. From this vantage we may be nearly certain that the poet considers him to possess extraordinary spiritual powers, in the guise of a fire which was hidden beneath his brows while he yet lived (line 11). And at last we appreciate the implications of the first line ("Now is the curtain fully parted"): Only after being deprived of his friend through death is the poet able to contemplate the flame of his friend's spirit, which finally enters into its own.

[24]   This elusive sonnet is concerned with worldly language and its degeneration, and with the restoration of an otherworldly, transcendent language. Lines 1–5 deal with language that will dispense with words; after historical time has ceased, things will be able to converse among themselves, without verbal mediation. A special ritual language which with a few humorous words sets the universe ringing or singing is mentioned in lines 6–8. This language depends in part on "brotherly foreknowing," and seems to adumbrate the mystical state of language without words, to be ushered in when history will have reached its end. Lines 9–10 may allude to social practices in which speechless trust counted rather than untrustworthy words when it came to a literal or figurative weighing of things. Lines 11–12 may evoke a collapse of social structures (*Gebilde*) cursed with degeneracy (cursing brings about the collapse). A final allusion to the human voice (line 14) introduces the motif of drunkenness and Eros, and with it a hint of redemption. At least drunkenness on the part of the poet and his friend is something fresh and delightful and intimate; and certainly transcendence glimmers in the mention of "early stars" (line 13).

L.4–5 Literally: "Meet each other as does the faithful watchmen's word the proscribed ring [band] of poetizing [verse-making] taciturnity." The German offers a figure which begins as a concrete image only to bleed teasingly into an abstraction.

L.10 *Vertrauen auf den Händen* "trusting on the hands" — Rather than the expected "trusting in the hands" (accusative); *stillen* can refer either to a cessation of sound or of movement; hence the quieting here applies either to "words" or to "scales."

L.11 *Todesmalen* "Signs of death"—The word as spoken also brings to mind *Todesmahlen* or "funeral meals." German Baroque funerary practices called for a formal meal to be held in the course of elaborate observances with which Benjamin would become familiar while preparing his *Habilitationsschrift* (*The Origin of the German Mourning Play*).

L.12 *Gebilde* "Structures"—A word with many shades of meaning, all sharing the idea of an entity which has acquired formal properties or been fashioned into something possessing a recognizable pattern or structure. A special usage is found in the writings of Benjamin's contemporaries (Carl Schmitt, György Lukács), according to which *Gebilde* refers to social constructs or institutions within the world as it is.

L.14 *in unsern Stimmen* "in our voices" — That is, in the voices of the poet and his friend.

[25]   The whole of this obscure sonnet seems to depend, once again, on the motif of stillness: Stillness of a chariot race carved in stone is followed by mention, in the tercets, of another unfinished, or suspended, race between the poet's Life and Death. Finally, there is the image of a boy (a Cupid figure) forever holding out a fruit before his master which will remind some readers of Keats's *Ode on a Grecian Urn*. Perhaps the poet's "rapid Autumn" is making a secret halt while these sonnets are being written down—and that, engaged in this way, he wards off dying by his own hand.

L.1 *rosigem Karneole* "in the rosy carnelian" — Carnelian is a semiprecious stone that was widely used in Roman times for rings and seals. Benjamin, who as a young man had already become something of a connoisseur of antique carved gems (see his *Berlin Chronicle*, notice 21), composed at least two other sonnets which bear on images carved in antique gems. He quotes the beginning of one, written after the start of the First World War, in the *Berlin Chronicle* (notice 21; the rest of the poem is lost). The other, dedicated to Jula Cohn, *Erweckung* ("Awakening"), addresses the image of a bride carved into an antique gem — whose sleep the poet dares to disturb when he finds himself sleepless and thinking only of her. (See "Appendix II: Other Sonnets.")

L.3–4 *eine Flucht . . . von Wagenlenkern Rossen* "a fleeing . . . of chariot riders steeds" — Chariot racing was a premier athletic event in the Greco-Roman world and many depictions are preserved on vases, wall reliefs, coins, and carved gems.

L.5 *im Kampf die Brüder schlüge* "in fighting overwhelms the brothers" — Literally, "[should] in fighting overwhelm the brothers."

Benjamin seems to be making some particular allusion, though to whom or what is hard to say. Normally his literary and cultural references are to standard things. Conceivably, these "brothers" are the mythical twins Castor and Pollux whom unnamed charioteers in the present image aspire to surpass in horsemanship.

L.6 *Die Kehr* "The turn" — Taken together with the mention of an aureole, we may envision shining from inside the carnelian some segment of the (oval) track of a hippodrome, the ancient Greco-Roman edifice designed for chariot races.

L.12 *der streng im Zucht hält* "which keeps me well in hand" — A reference to "me" (*mich*) seems understood.

[26]

L.1 *geliebte Kinder* "beloved children" (line 2) — They may be identified with Fritz Heinle and Rika Seligson.

L.12–13 *vor dem Innern des Gartens* "before the inner garden" — Literally, "before the interior of the garden."

L.14 *In das die . . . Andacht wies* "Into which . . . Reverence showed the way" — In a reversal of the original expulsion of Adam and Eve from Eden, the lovers are now invited to enter a new Paradise watched over by angels without weapons. Immediately before, these two had sensed earthly Love falling "humbly silent" (line 6) within themselves and had recognized sorrow as ripe fruit associated with "past sweet kisses" (lines 9–11); perhaps their stay in the new Paradise is to be a chaste one.

[27]   This sonnet is one which appears determined to cling to secrets. Still, it is likely that "those remembered" is a reference to Fritz Heinle and Rika Seligson.

Let us suppose further that Yearning — the poet's — finds itself to be out of step with ever-ongoing living and dying. The interrogative rhetoric of lines 5–8 may be meant to elevate Heinle and Seligson above whatever will happen after they have died: The tale of "those remembered" (remembered by the poet) sounds nowhere; the bells which do sound are not for his friends but join together strange couples; and children, if they are to be comforted, will not be comforted by the poet or by those for whom he grieves. The last lines of the sonnet introduce fresh perplexities with the appearance of "the Soul" (whose we do not know). It is interesting that "those remembered and those loved" do not ascend into Heaven but descend into the gloom of a pagan afterlife.

L.6 *den Gefeierten* "those [who are] remembered" —*Feiern* means to celebrate or commemorate a person or an event.

L.7 *wen fugt er frühe* "whom do [swarming bells] too soon unite" (lines 6-7) — Here *fugt* implies *zusammenfügt*.

L.11–14 A fin-de-siècle atmosphere surrounds the figures evoked in these closing lines; one sees them shrouded in robes and descending solemnly and ceremoniously into murky twilight.

L.14 *Vor ihrem Blick* "Before their gaze" —Referring to the two who have descended to Hades; but the phrase can also be rendered with "Before her gaze," so as to refer to the Soul, personified.

[28]

L.7–8 Lines alluding to the deaths of Fritz Heinle and Rika Seligson, who took their own lives inhaling gas from an oven; "fetid life" must allude to the atmosphere of wartime jubilation which overtook Germany in August 1914. The grieving poet praises the moral composure which led his friends to end their lives "without anguish or delay." And despite the seeming violence of their self-destruction, he insists on the gentleness of the act; it was a fitting response to the violence which broke out "beneath blind midnight's triumph." "Breathed out" corresponds only roughly to the German *geräumt* (literally, "cleared out").

L.11 *der Euch je gelang* "which always brought good fortune" — Literally, "which always succeeded for You."

L.12 A most peculiar line. One misses a direct object (*Euch*) and in any case would sooner have: "Nie *überzeugen* [Euch] Lied und Freund zurück" ("Never do song and friend convince [You] [to come] back"). Yet Benjamin has written "überlegen." As a reflexive verb, "überlegen" can mean "to reflect on" or "to ponder"; hence the translation here, with reflexiveness and direct object assumed.

[29]   Sonnet 29 marks a departure from "rough facture." Its syntax continues throughout to dovetail with the lines, while appeals to the Christ-like deceased friend accumulate. The poem scans quite easily.

L.1 *Du Schlummernder* "Thou slumberer" — The addressee is the poet's deceased friend.

L.3 *Erlöster* "[thou] who frees" — *Erlöster* means, with reference to a person, "one [who has been] freed or redeemed." The translation assumes instead *Erlöser* ("redeemer, liberator"). Here requirements for rhyming may once again have skewed the meaning.

L.9 *Engel des Friedens* "Angel of peace" — These words suggest that Fritz Heinle was a pacifist.

L.13–14 *Bringer neuer Huld … unsrer Schuld* "Bringer of new grace … our guilt" — The poet's friend, who has been all things to all people, is now assigned a Christ-like role. Perhaps the guilt referred to in the last line of the sonnet belongs to those who were close to Heinle and Rika Seligson — two who, as it were, died for the sins of the world.

[30]   In this sonnet the master-idea is Resurrection. The poet establishes an intimate relation between his word — his breath — and the hands of his friend, which he imagines emerging from the grave. The resurrection of the poet's words causes his song to crowd like colored lanterns ("iridescent beacons") into the "joyous places" of those hands. Beginning with line 6, his words become like butterflies. The butterfly-words seek a safe harbor in late summer flowers, where instead a scentless, newly risen aster may be waiting for them, its face turned toward the sky and away from earthly things. Words will be brought into relation with butterflies again in Benjamin's *Berlin Childhood* ("Butterfly hunt").

L.3 *der schon verdorrte* "the dessicated" — Literally, "the already dessicated."

L.6 *des Liedes farbige Fanale* "iridescent beacons of my music" (line 5) — Literally, "colored beacons [lanterns] of the [my] song."

L.12 *schürt* "still smolders" — Normally, *schüren* is a transitive verb meaning "to fuel a fire," or figuratively, to fuel a conflict or to stir up some negative feeling or emotion.

L.13 *ersteht* "rising" — In the Christian context, rising from the dead.

[31]   With its references to butterflies (line 4) and to the Christ-like resurrection of an unnamed man, this sonnet continues to play with motifs introduced in Sonnet 30. Now it is suggested that life as we know it shall end, following the friend's resurrection — and disappearance — and that a dubious sort of Paradise will take its place. There will be perpetual sunlight and a disappearance of troublesome things such as dark seasons and sexual entanglements, but so, too, will the friend and saviour have disappeared: "The very ground shall know his step no more / And of his voice no more the air."

L.3–4 *Überschwang des Sturmes* "brimful storm" — Literally, "exuberance [overflow, superabundance] of the storm."

L.11 *Sein Name . . . entglitt* "escaped his name" — An especially jarring momentary shift of tense, from future to simple past.

L.12 *Und nie mehr Liebende* "never more shall lover" — The lover is female.

L.14 *auferstanden* "is risen" — That is, risen from the dead and ascended to Heaven.

[32]   As the sun is setting, the poet follows a path which was made by the footsteps of his friend, now dead, and comes upon a clearing where the ground is sacred and not to be trod upon ("the ready place," line 9). It may be that this spot symbolizes for him the mysterious way his friend's steps left the earth (see also sonnets 31 and 58). Here, in this place, in the deepening twilight, he senses that his own "refuge lies ahead" (line 14) in darkness to come.

L.7 *braunen* "earthen" (line 6) — Literally, "brown."

L.7–8 *grade Unendlichkeit* "endlessness unbending" (line 8) — Literally, "straight [not crooked] endlessness [infiniteness]"

L.13 *dem Horizonte* "to far distant sky" (lines 12–13) — Literally, "to the horizon."

L.14 *mir erscheint mein Hort* "my refuge lies ahead" — Literally, "my refuge appears to [in front of] me."

[33]   Sonnet 33 is the first in a series of four (nos. 33–36) in which the poet adopts a confessional tone in order to reveal the intensity and erotic coloring of his feelings for his friend. Benjamin himself was one who loved secrets and took pleasure in thinking about when or if he would give one up. And he was given to preparing surprises for friends (see *Berlin Childhood*, "The fever"). At the conclusion of the present sonnet the poet will divulge to the reader a secret which has been hidden in this series of poems, namely, that he so loved his friend that the friend *was* his life. And yet his own daughter, Love, is not to learn the secret until the poet is on his deathbed.

A puzzling being is Love: If she represents the love of the poet for his deceased friend, then she did not know herself for what she was. Having to wait until she reads these sonnets to find out suggests an oddly circuitous state of affairs. This may be Benjamin's way of representing his own circuitous working out of the significance for him of his friendship with Heinle — which came to him fully perhaps only after the latter's death. Meanwhile the question posed in lines 6–7 ("Why do I wait . . . to yield to her what should stay hers . . . ?") is otherwise left unanswered, the rhetoric of lines 8–11 ("Here then is my reason . . . ") notwithstanding.

See also Sonnet 56, which once again provides the poet with a child.

L.5 *dieses Buch* "this book" — Presumably a book containing Benjamin's sonnets. Love has known of it since childhood, but she seems never to have opened it and looked inside: Her acquaintance was strictly superficial.

L.6 Literally: "Why do I postpone [handing] it [over] until [my] death has come?

L.10 *Reben* "vines" — That is, grapevines.

L.14 *sein Leben* "his life" — A sudden unprepared allusion to the poet's friend.

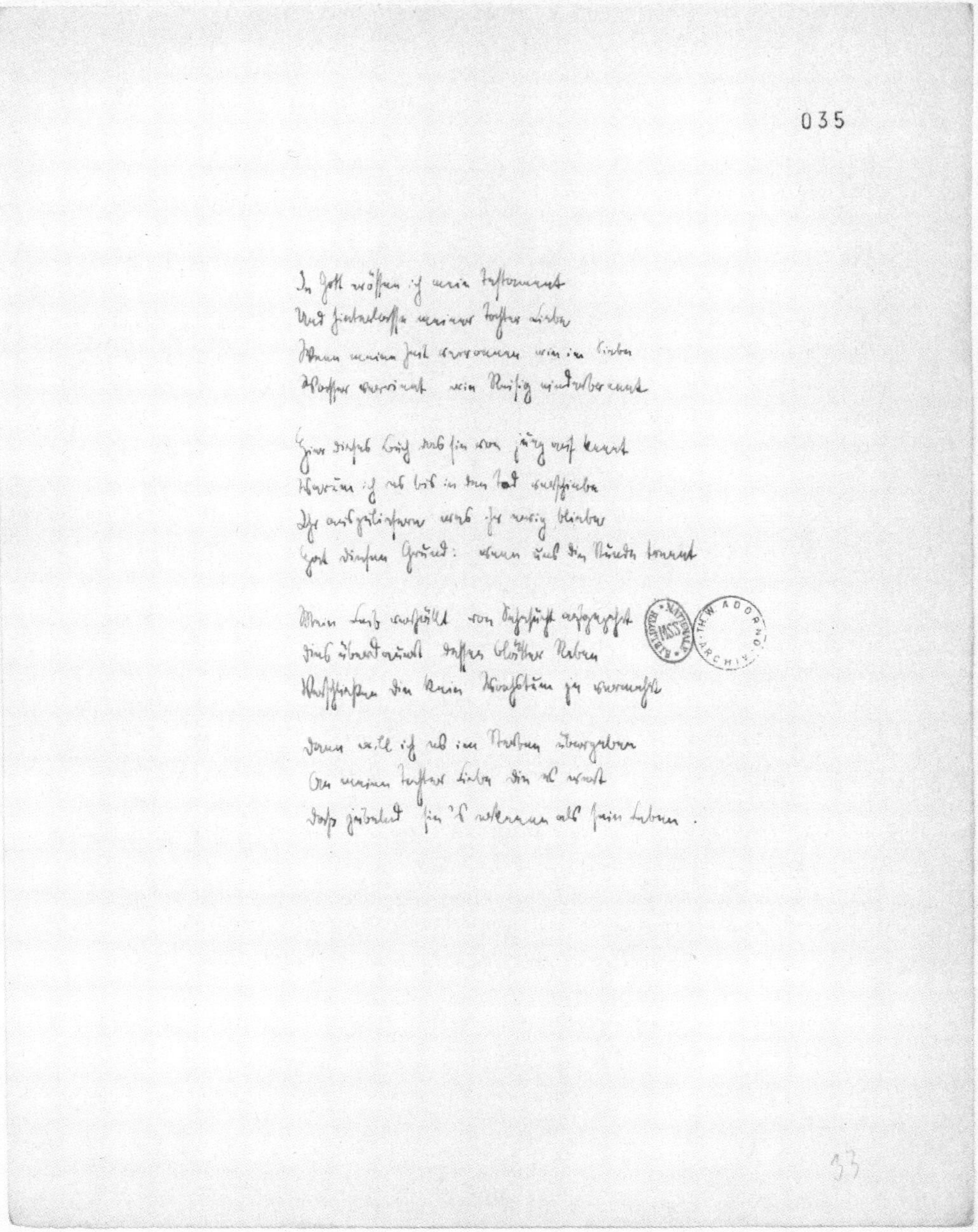

In Gott wähnen ich mein Testament

Benjamin's fair copy of Sonnet 33
(Akademie der Künst, Berlin, Walter Benjamin Archiv, Sign.: 253/35)

[34]   In its first eleven lines, Sonnet 34 elaborates a meditative moment in the present life of the poet—a moment during which the dead friend assumes a spectral presence. The second tercet draws on a particular memory to conjure a different moment, one of startling intimacy, from when both young men were still alive. Essentially lyric in character, this sonnet is little indebted to "rough facture" (and yet Benjamin still does not provide end-rhymes which are convincingly easy or unproblematic).

L.9 *mein Freund* "O friend" — See the note for line 1 of the next sonnet.

L.10 *Ich taste wie der Schläfer* "Like one asleep whose hand looks" — Poetic license on the part of the translator: "In dark hours I grope for thee like one asleep who feels for the wreath in his own hair" makes for a literal translation of the passage.

L.13 *aus dem schwarzen Rund* "from within the midnight throng" — Literally, "from within the black round [of dancers]."

[35]   Here as in Sonnet 33 the motif of the secret is paramount, and once again the culmination is a delayed confession of the poet's love for his friend. Now, however, his confession is more explicit: Sexual feelings are part of the love. Even though his friend inquires and seems to wish to know the truth (line 1) he may not share such feelings, and if he does not, this would seem reason enough for the poet to hide his own.

L.1 *den Freund* "my friend" — Literally, "the friend." The poet's friend refers to himself indirectly, and ambiguously: In German one may politely acknowledge a same-sex relationship by referring to "den [mein, dein] Freund" ("the [my, your] friend").

L.2 *was sich ... staute* "what had knotted been" — Literally, "what had been stopped [clogged] up."

L.4 *das Kristall der Triebe* "the crystal of the drives" — The poet's erotic urge had been kept in a solid crystalline state and did not express itself.

L.8 *Verstohlnes Ja* "a surreptitious 'Yes'" — The poet answers his friend's question — but only for himself.

L.11 Literally: "The hand which cannot decide whether or not to give itself to the friend."

Benjamin's fair copy of Sonnet 34
(Akademie der Künst, Berlin, Walter Benjamin Archiv, Sign.: 253/36)

L.12 *hat er ergriffen* "is by him seized"—That is, seized by the friend in death. From beyond the grave the friend—more cruel now—will take the poet's hand and compel him to spill his rhymes in public. This conceit notwithstanding, Benjamin is not known to have made a great effort to publish his sonnets.

L.13–14 Literally: "So that it [the hand] must spill the heart which loved in secret, in rhymes."

[36]   The setting of the sonnet must be Freiburg im Breisgau, that subalpine university town in the far southwestern corner of Germany where Walter Benjamin and Fritz Heinle first met in April 1913. In this sonnet, the poet remembers that his confessional impulse was strong even in those days, and that it nearly broke free in the presence of his friend.

L.1–7 A bold realization of "rough facture," of syntactic displacement and delay: Here "when" (at the beginning of the second quatrain) refers back to the first line: "How flaming was the breath of days." Several large liberties have been taken in translating these lines.

L.7 *schürzen* "store up"—Literally, "to gather up [one's skirts]" or to "bind [in a knot]."

L.8 Consists of two short sentences—making a foil for the extended "rough facture" of lines 1–7; *die Stadt* "the town"—Oddly, the town is now referred to in the third person after having been apostrophized.

L.9 *das Laub* "the trees"—Literally, "the foliage."

L.10 Literally: "In talk, the rushing of the river still whispers."

L.11 *die nicht forscht* "which does not guess"—Literally, "does not look into [or investigate]" or "does not fathom."

L.12 *leiser* "quieter"—There is a furtive change of feeling in the poet, whereas the warming mood in his friend is undisguised; *im Geliebten* "in the loved one"—Masculine. The word implies that one friend is in some sense the more active while the other, "the loved one," is the more passive.

L.14 Normal word order would be: "Das Wort das nächtlich haust bei Liebenden," which is the sense provided by the translation. Benjamin's contorted order, impossible to carry over into unrhymed English, hints at how inhibited "the loved one" is: That word-stream issuing from one friend blows away from

236

the mouth of the other the single word which ought to be part of the intimate nightly life of those who love, and so it remains unuttered.

[37]

　L.1 *uns will die Stadt ... sein* "ours the town ... shall be" — Here "ours" refers to the poet and his friend Fritz Heinle.

　L.3 *wird ... vernommen* "but seem like" — Literally, "will be perceived as [taken for]."

　L.7 *wie Kerzen glommen* "did glow like tapers" — Yet another disconcerting shift of tense. One is tempted to impute to Benjamin a veritable programme of temporal derangement, in the spirit of Baudelaire's "dérèglement de tous les sens."

　L.7–8 *Dort fangen Äste ... den Tag um unsre Stirnen ein* "There branches ... seize outer day around our brows" — But it could also be that the branches merely shut in or enclose the outer day around the two friends' brows.

　L.14 *Und ... in dem Münster* "And ... in the minster" — Like the preceding sonnet, no. 37 seems to have to do with the charming university town of Freiburg im Breisgau, where Benjamin first met Fritz Heinle. After his glancing personal allusion in lines 1–2, the poet leads readers through a suggestive thicket of nature-images all the while scattering clues for our interpretation of them as a species of architecture. Increasingly we understand that the "blessed joy" of returning to the town means that the two young men will once again find themselves in the forest-like depths of Freiburg Cathedral. The concluding images of a dark sun in its zenith and a dark midday align this sonnet with nos. 10, 14, 21, 42, 43, 47, 49, 54, and 72, since the motif of light within darkness — or even light which is made *from* darkness — is important in all of them.

[38]　This sonnet, organized around cryptic references to summer and to winter, and perhaps childhood and adulthood, does not seem willing to yield whatever hermetic meaning it had for Benjamin.

　L.1 *Märkische Stadt* "the marchland town" — The allusion may be to Brandenburg, the principal town of the Mark of Brandenburg, or to some other within the region surrounding Berlin.

　L.5–6 These stubbornly obscure lines may touch upon an episode recalled by

Benjamin in *Berlin Childhood*, in "Pfaueninsel und Glienecke": a child, hastening from the Pfaueninsel ("Peacock Island," lying in the Havel River near the Wannsee) looks in the windows of a mock castle and learns from the way they reflect the sinking sun that he will not enter the castle and (in effect) become king. It may be that here Benjamin is addressing his childhood self in the second person as "du."

L.6 *Abbild* "image" — In the sense of a reflected image.

L.8 Several words are indecipherable in Benjamin's MS; the reading given by the editors of the Suhrkamp edition of the Sonnets remains conjectural.

L.9 *Gestirn* "star" — A shining heavenly body; the moon, the sun, or a planet.

L.11 *Riegen* "ranks" — Literally, "squads [teams, sections]."

L.13 *dichten* "clustered" — Literally, "dense" or "thick."

[39]

L.2 *Gericht* "Judgment" — The ordinary meaning is "tribunal," another sense being the judgment handed down by a court. At the Last Judgment ("das jüngste Gericht") when earthly time has come to an end, God shall judge mankind and usher in eternity.

L.5 *Pavilion* "pleasure garden" — Literally, "pavilion," usually a garden house set within a park.

L.6 *Ein Gesicht* "One single vision" — The more usual meaning of *Gesicht* is "face." Here it probably means the power to see things as though they were really before one's eyes. Benjamin has capitalized *Ein* for emphasis, contrary to standard practice. In so doing he may be alluding to the effort of mystics such as Abraham Abulafia to understand God's oneness. (Hölderlin, Rilke, and George all capitalized this word occasionally in their poems.)

L.9 *Wir alle liebten Einen* "One we all did love" — *Einen* ("One") has been capitalized, contrary to standard practice. The unnamed man who was loved by all the rest and has been carried off is of course the poet's friend.

L.11 *er ihm ferne hielt von* "he kept from us" — Literally, "he kept him [each one] away from."

L.12 Literally: "Our joy was almost thoroughly ripened and rural [sylvan, pastoral, Arcadian]." The final word of the line (*ländlich*) seems farfetched.

L.13 *was uns verklagte* "which did accuse us" — The motifs of guilt and judging were introduced in lines 2-3.

[40]

L.4 *Der Horizont* "The distant sky" — Literally, "the horizon"; *überronnen* "Overrun" — Carries a military connotation, as when forces succeed in displacing an enemy from the field. The field of the sky has been overrun with red.

L.9 "Sich aus dem Staube machen" is an everyday expression meaning "to beat it" or "to hurry away" (raising dust in the process). Here it is amalgamated with something mystical, a sort of time-dust, literally "the dust of this time."

L.14 Literally, " . . . thy happiness must borrow from the earlier ones." The line is problematic. Its grammar points to "evening" (line 13) as the referent, so as to yield "earlier evenings," since there is no plural form for the word *Glück* (line 14). And yet the line wants to be read as saying: "From now on thy happiness must borrow from earlier happinesses."

[41] The sonnet is cast in an imprecise trochaic meter of irregular feet (between 7 and 10 syllables in length). In it, the poet addresses his personified Soul, envisioning for her a scene rather like Christian Communion with its table and the goblet of wine. Instead of the blood of Christ, however, this wine shall be full of the poet's friend. For some readers the final conceit (lines 11–14) may smack more of Wagner — what with the poet's Soul ready to drink a deadly potion to be at one with his deceased friend.

L.6–8 Literally: "Opaque feathers which trail downward [like] shedding [falling, dropping] leaves strip [denude, deprive] you of the Present." Benjamin's intransitive use of *blätternd* (line 8) to suggest trees shedding leaves is his own.

[42] The first lines of this sonnet: "Those hours which contain the Figure / Have expired in the house of dreams" would be used as an epigraph for the "Souterrain"

section of Benjamin's collection *One-way Street* (issued in 1928). There he recounts a dream he had "during a night of despair," and in which he is reunited with his lost friend, the "first comrade of his school days"—a powerfully emotional experience. But upon waking, he recognizes his friend as a corpse embedded in the wall of the basement of his own "house of life" ("Haus des Lebens"); no one who shall live in this house will ever resemble the dead friend in any way.

In the sonnet, the poet constructs his "house of dreams" from starry and planetary elements, surrounding it with an atmosphere of bright and icy interstellar cold. Those hours with dreams that "contain the Figure" have "expired," and yet the friend ("he") will return suddenly as flaring light (line 14).

L.3 *erkaufen* "obtain"—In the sense of buy or purchase; can also mean "to bribe or subborn."

L.7 *kalten* "icy"—Literally, "cold."

L.8. *roten* "bright red"—Literally, "red."

L.10–11 Possibly the seven rooms of the poet's "house of dreams" are overseen by the seven planets of classical astrology.

L.14 *Er entfacht ward* "he flared"—Literally, "he was kindled." An unexpected return to the friend, the "Figure" (line 1). An alternative reading for the line: "It flared . . . ," referring to "beam" (line 12).

[43]

L.7 *grollte* "curled up"—An odd shortening of *gerollte* to facilitate the rhyme scheme.

L.11 *in geheimsten Ringe* "inside a most mysterious ring"—To be taken in the geometric sense of a circle, whereas in Sonnet 24 Benjamin spoke of a "proscribed ring [band]" of poets who make poems from silence.

L.12 *in ihrem Licht* "in their light"—Referring to the poet's thoughts. Can also be translated as "in its light," referring to the light of the poet's new sun.

L.13 *wunderbar* "strangely"—Can also mean "wonderfully" or "miraculously."

L.14 *Bist du* "Thou art"—An unprepared reference to the poet's friend: Just as the sun maintains shadows, so the poet's thinking maintains his friend's existence—as a shadow of empty things.

[44]

L.2 *Stern der dich ... rief* "star which called thee" — The star which determines one's destiny.

L.3 *ins liebste Leben* "into my dearest life" — A likely reference to the poet's Soul, yet to be named.

L.4 The poet is being stolen from life by "rapid arrows" which do him no harm — dying will leave him unharmed. It may be that because his dearest friend has died, he, too, is fated to die. The second quatrain as well as the first tercet of the sonnet present images of the poet's Soul taking leave of his body and of things past.

L.7 *Ward ... reiner Schein* "did ... turn to purest semblance" — See the note to line 14, Sonnet 10.

L.8 *im Abend* "in evening light" — Literally, "in the evening."

L.10 *den schwarzen Sammet* "the soft black velvet" — Literally, "the black velvet."

L.11 *decken* "cover" — Can have the sense of "to protect [by covering]."

L.13 *erstarren* "grows rigid" — Can also have the sense of "freeze" or "are chilled."

L.14 *du bist traumlos zu gewahren* "thou art dreamless to discern" — Can be construed to mean that the friend is himself not part of any dream (as the poet perceives him) or that the poet is able to discern his friend without dreaming. However it may be, the friend has transcended the dangerous realm of images and become more real for the poet.

[45] This sonnet is cast in a thumping Schilleresque meter of dactyls and trochees, with lines varying in length between 12 and 16 syllables. Certain mannerisms — for example the interpolation of an exclamatory "see" in the penultimate line and references to "the Beautiful one" (a male; lines 1 and 4) — also recall Schiller. Benjamin himself did not care for Schiller; several passages in *Berlin Childhood* cite lines by the famous poet in order to mock the *bildungsbürgerliche* pieties of Benjamin's childhood milieu (see "Tiergarten" and "Two riddles"). The second quatrain introduces a contrasting, Judeo-Christian element when God himself is

addressed with "O Lord" and then as the "Desolate one" (referring to the abandoned Jesus). Yet another figure is the poet's Soul, addressed familiarly in the first quatrain and later referred to in the third person. Sorrowing goes on in both the poet and his Soul whether or not they share their griefs with each other.

L.5 *Weinen und Stöhnen* "weeping and groaning"—That is, the poet's own weeping and groaning.

L.14 *Ihre* "Her"—In Benjamin's MS there is a marked break in the middle of the line, and "Ihre," the word following, is capitalized; *entbrannten* "flaring"—Literally, "flared [kindled]."

[46]

L.5 *wißt* "know Ye"—Those addressed with the second-person plural are the poet's deceased friend and his friend's lover.

L.7 *Ich bin und war* "I am and was"—The first use of the first-person singular in this sonnet. But it seems that a single voice is speaking throughout the sonnet, who in the beginning referred to himself in the third person as "Ruler Death."

L.10 *schwesterlichen* "sisterhoodly"—Literally, "sisterly."

L.14 *schmalen Mund* "narrow mouths"—The two lovers are dead; their mouths are drawn tight. It is Death who bestows a final grace upon them, having shown them benevolence all during their fated voyage on the ship of Love.

[47]

L.2 *die schläfert es im Raume* "who drowsy grow in space"—possibly an image of constellations in the night sky.

L.3 *Netzt unser Lager Feuer* "Our couch shall wetted be by fire"—Sometimes the verb *netzen* (to wet, to moisten) is used with "tears" for cheeks wet from weeping.

L.4 *Herz der...Freundin* "girl's heart"—The heart is that of someone's particular friend or lover.

L.5 *in dem breiten Baume* "in the spreading tree"—Literally, "in the broad tree."

L.8 *am schwarzen Saume* "by the black bed"—That is, by the edge of a garden bed. But the usual meaning of *Saum* is "hem" or "trimming" and hence one thinks as well of funerary decor.

L.14 *all sein Licht* "all his light" — Benjamin often reserves the final lines of a sonnet for an oblique allusion to his deceased friend and occasionally, as here, the unexpected reference is accompanied by a sudden shift in tense. But *sein* might as well refer to "beam" (line 12). The meaning of Sonnet 47 remains in doubt: Still, let us suppose two different fires or sources of light — one stirring from the girl's unquiet grave and her quarreling dream, threatening escape, the other belonging to her lover — and that in some way the latter can bring peace to the former. In his *Berlin Chronicle* (notice 12) Benjamin recalled that Fritz Heinle and Rika Seligson were interred in separate cemeteries; that it had not been possible for them to be buried in the same grave even though they had taken their lives together.

[48]

L.1 Translating pronoun references in this sonnet presented a challenge. Without taking many liberties it did not seem possible to convey coherently the actions that are described in it. One such liberty has been to personify Memory ("das Erinnern") as feminine. The point of this and other pronoun alterations has been to avoid unclear (neutral) pronoun references in the translation.

L.3 *Die junge Flut* "her young flood" — The flood of Memory; literally, "the young flood." Subsequent pronoun references to the flood are translated with "her" as though these referred directly back to Memory (line 1).

L.4 Literally: "Within the straitenend vale which for her sake [the flood's] did remember joy."

L.9–10 *Doch harret ... an der Vergängnis stetigen Gesetzen* "And yet ... clinging to the constant laws of Pastness" — The controlling metaphor of this sonnet likens the grieving poet's memory to a flow of water; memory is subject to the laws of time (and of forgetting) just as a river obeys gravity and must at last lose itself in the sea.

The verb form *harren* + *an* is not recognized in standard dictionaries (Duden, Grimm). Here it may have the sense of "to cling to." Or it may simply mean "to wait for" or "to stand in attendance on."

[49]

L.1 *Das war ich wußt es wohl* "It was . . . well I knew" — The opening hints at another dream-sonnet. In this dream the poet feels himself close to Fritz Heinle and Rika Seligson as they embark on the final voyage.

L.6 *Zum schwarzen Schein* "[to] a shining blackness" — See the note for Sonnet 10, line 14, and also that for Sonnet 21, lines 7–8; *aus erschlossenem Spind* "from the unlocked panel" — Literally, "from the unlocked [thrown open] cabinet [locker, wardrobe]."

L.8 *Ihr seid in mir verwahrt* "In me are You kept safe" — In Benjamin's MS extra space precedes these words, creating for them an optical buffer.

L.9 The poet imagines himself to be a staff of domestics belonging to an old-fashioned aristocratic household and in the service of the Spirit of his dead friends.

L.11 The Spirit and the poet (as its household) are just as closely mated as are the poet and his verses (see next line).

L.12 Literally: "As the poet is conscious of himself in his own song." Thus does the poet — Walter Benjamin — become embodied in these verses and, as it were, enter into the service of his dead friends.

[50]

L.2 *Bram* "topsail" — A nautical term for the mast above the topmast, its sails, or its rigging; more generally, something which is raised above adjacent parts or structures.

L.3 *Doch der* "Which however" — The reference is to Time's topsail; *in seinem Spiegel* "in its glass" — That is, in the glass of Time; *wiederzeigend* "by reflection" — Benjamin's nonce-word; literally, "showing [something] again."

L.4 *ihn* "him" — The masculine pronouns in Sonnet 50 are troublesome. Here, "him" most likely refers back to personified Remembering — the poet's remembering — in defiance of grammar. Remembering would then persist as the masculine subject for the rest of the sonnet. Or we may consider "him" an unprepared reference to the poet, to the one who is doing the remembering.

L.7 Literally: "Until he consolingly and with the concession 'Yes' [made off with all the images]."

L.8 *der Vergebung stumme Hymne* "his mute forgiving hymn" — The poet (Remembering) silently forgives his deceased friend — who perhaps must be forgiven for dying and leaving the poet (Remembering) alone.

L.10 *Befreiter Blick* "His gaze now freed" — The poet's gaze is liberated after he gives up those images and signs of his friend which he had been guarding as keepsakes.

L.11 *Reis* "fresh growth" — Can also mean "offspring" or "scion."

L.14 *Kommender Kinder* "Of coming children" — The poet may be vowing to create works from the inspiration left him by his friend — out of the permanence left by his friend's absence. Benjamin's renunciation of other memories and his turn to the special Name and his praising of it recalls the first sonnet and provides a suitable ending for his planned series of fifty poems.

[51]   The second of the three groups of Heinle sonnets as Benjamin preserved them begins with Sonnet 51 and extends through no. 59. The majority of these are examples of his smoother — one is tempted to say his more conventional — expression; none of them is truly obscure as are many of the sonnets in his main set of fifty (nos. 1–50) as well as some of those in the third group (nos. 60–73). No fewer than four of the sonnets in the second group mention characters from Greek mythology by name, whereas pagan references in the remaining groups are comparatively peripheral and generalized. These sonnets also exhibit more variability in their choice of rhyme scheme and meter. If anything, the second group displays a more secure poetic technique than do the other two, whereas these latter provide evidence of a more inward exploration and greater openness to risk. It may be that the second group reflects an early phase of Benjamin's sonnet enterprise.

L.1 *Maße* "measures" — The poet's verse measures, his meters.

L.3 *zu ihm* "to him" — A reference to the poet's deceased friend, whom he (actually his Soul) seeks and hopes to find through writing this sonnet. L.8. Lichtung "clearing" — That is, a clearing in the forest.

L.10 *Plutos* "Pluto"—The Lord of the Underworld is meant (Greek: Plouton) but the ancient god of wealth is named (Ploutos). Conceptually related, they may have been one and the same divinity originally and have sometimes been confused.

L.11 *den kürzern Pfad* "The shorter passage" — Literally, "the shorter path": the pair of tercets with which sonnets in the Petrarchan pattern conclude.

L.14 *der letzte Reim* "the final rhyme" — The form of the sonnet corresponds with actions from the story of Orpheus and his failed rescue of Euridice from Hades. The poet's last rhyme causes the sonnet to be over, just as Euridice must vanish when Orpheus looks back. Fritz Heinle was a poet and a fitting Orpheus figure — but Benjamin himself is writing this sonnet, and draws our attention to his act of writing. He seems both to identify himself with his friend — becoming one with him, a second poet — and vainly to seek him: If he ends his sonnet, his link with the friend will be gone.

[52]

L.2 *sie* "she" — In retrospect, the reference belongs to "Beauty" and not "sorrow."

L.7 *Schein* "Semblance" — For Benjamin a metaphysical term; see the note for Sonnet 10, line 14.

L.10 *Sprache taugt ihr nicht* "Words will [not] suit her" — Whether the poet is thinking of language as it may be used to speak of Beauty, or used *by* Beauty herself — or in both these ways — is left open. The line, impossible to translate closely, speaks of the contrasting worlds of night and day, which are also the worlds of semblance and of truth according to Benjamin's aesthetics.

L.11 *blendend* "blinding" — Has the sense of "dazzling" or "deceiving." To undo these tresses is blinding for anyone who dares to try; Beauty cannot be undone — analyzed — without cost. An impersonal passive construction leaves room for Helen herself as the undoer.

L.11 *ihr Geflecht* "her tresses" — Can also mean "her weaving."

L.12 *deiner Schönheit* "to thy beauty" — The final tercet brings in the poet's friend, and it is the friend's moral beauty which the poet commemorates. Here as elsewhere Benjamin insists on the nobility of Fritz Heinle's suicide in protest of war.

L.13 *Jugendleben* — Left untranslated; Benjamin had come to conceive of Youth (*Jugend*) as a distinct form of existence or "life" (*Leben*) with its own metaphysics. Fritz Heinle was its finest instantiation.

[53]   Benjamin's taste for allegory and ballad style is given free rein in verses of iambic tetrameter. Outwardly, the poem conforms to the Petrarchan sonnet with its pairs of quatrains and tercets and in its rhyme scheme. A relatively free translation is meant to ensure the popular narrative tone of the original.

L.1 *mit solcher Fracht* "with such strange freight" — Literally, "with such freight."

L.3 *der Name Herz* "the name of Heart" — Presumably this ship carries for its principal cargo the poet's heart.

L.5 *du siehst* "you see" — The reader is being familiarly addressed.

L.14 *verfällt dem Meer* "falls to the sea" — With an indirect object, verfallen has the meaning of "to fall to [by right, by law]."

[54]

L.6 *ich nichts verflöße* "that I let nothing flow away" — Literally, "so that I vanish [flow away] nothing." An unorthodox construction by means of which *verfließen* functions as a transitive verb.

L.7 *Verfährt mein innrer Strom* "my inner stream does stray" — Another unorthodox construction; here a verb normally reflexive is used intransitively. Benjamin's strange use of familiar verbs creates a grammatical equivalent for disoriented feelings.

L.11 *ertaubten* "numbed" — Can also mean "deafened."

L.13 *Am Haupt des Jahrs* "Upon the Year's Head" — An allusion to Rosh Hashanah, a holiday which marks the beginning of the Jewish year and whose Hebrew name means "head of the year." Benjamin offers a daringly literal image of this head with its scars.

L.14 *Des flammenden Augustes* "of an August gone to flame" — A reference to August 1914, and to the death of Fritz Heinle. (In that year the Jewish New Year fell on September 21.)

[55]

L.3–4 Literally: "And pays more dearly for his dull colors / Than do others for their rich, full ones."

L.7 Literally: "As over heavy grave-markers [plates]."

L.11 This line contains oblique references. "Sie" ("they") refers to the poet's eyes (not to his tears). "Es" ("müßens"="müßen es") refers back to "Bildnis" ("likeness," line 2; translated as "the thing"). And "aus dem Innern" (literally, "from the interior") is to be read as "from deep inside [me]."

L.12 Literally: "With desire [lust] drunk with yearning." Benjamin's newly minted adjective is tautological.

L.13 *Urbild*—Left untranslated. Normally meaning "archetype" or "epitome," the word is best taken here to mean "primal image."

L.14 In the German, the line expresses doubling by means of mirroring. The sonnet ends by uniting the poet and his deceased friend in a visual/verbal *Urbild* in which each mirrors the other.

[56] The sonnet centers upon a mysterious child who was presumably born to the poet when his friend died—on a day "full of danger full of blood" (line 4). This child stands for the poet's memory of the friend. Such memory is burdensome, even treacherous (lines 10–11) and it seems more to depend on the absent friend than on the helpless poet (lines 13–14). Mention of "seven years ago" (line 1) would suggest 1921 as the date of composition (Heinle having committed suicide in August 1914). But probably the number should not be taken literally.

L.2 In Benjamin's MS there is a space before *ohne*, which is then capped.

L.6 *Wenn unsrer Lippen...paaren* "When our lips mate"—Those who forget themselves and too ardently kiss are the poet and his Life, which would mean the poet and unspecified third parties (the poet and anyone but his friend).

L.7 *Spiel* "play"—Suggests verbal hinting as well as physical maneuvering or playfulness.

L.7 *Wenn wir...waren* "When...we are"—The use of the past tense in the German may only have served to supply an end-rhyme.

L.14 *von seinem Bilde* "by his image"—A reference to the poet's deceased friend.

[57] In this sonnet it is implied that the poet no longer feels such pain as once he did. And yet he imagines ways his pain might come back to him and achieve

a homecoming not unlike Odysseus's (see also sonnets 54 and 62). In some vague way the poet's returning pain is imagined to be his friend: it is almost as if the friend were "a pain" in and of himself who travels with the help of ill-humor and woe (line 3) and knows his way into the inmost chamber of the poet's heart.

L.3 *Dein Meer war Mißmut* "Ill-humor was thine ocean" — An allusion to Fritz Heinle's darker moods (see also sonnets 1, 6, 8, and 22).

L.11 *diesen alten Leib* "this wasted body" — Literally, "this old body."

L.13–14 Literally: "Thou mightest grope thy way following [building] plans well known to thee into the chamber of my tears."

[58] Sonnet 58 alternates lines of 3.5 and 2 iambic feet — an intriguing scheme all the more effective in concert with unforced end-rhymes. Benjamin may be emulating Goethe, master of the concise lyric poem (see, for example, "Gefunden," which also employs short iambic lines). Then, too, Baudelaire had made use of very similar metrics in a poem which Benjamin translated in these years ("A une mendiante rousse").

L.4 *ein Schein* "a phantom" — The German possesses philosophic gravity (see the note to Sonnet 10, line 14).

L.5 *Minne* "Love's courting" — In the strict sense refers to medieval courtly love. This "Minne" must refer to the poet's courting of his deceased friend's spirit.

L.9–14 These lines are freely rendered. Even so, they do not preserve an ingenious interleaving found in the German and shown in the following English version: "And so thou didst escape me / Til I learned [that] / To flawless pleas alone / Does Nature disclose / And only to steps away from earth / The blessed trace."

L.13 *entrückten Tritten* "steps away from earth" — Literally, "removed steps" or "steps carried off [snatched away]; figuratively, "transported [enraptured] steps." For similar images, see sonnets 31 and 32.

[59] The poet, being in no easy relation with the words he needs to do justice to his deceased friend, contrasts winged ones that came from the gods with ease and swiftness — when the latter willed it — with others that obey only his deceased friend and the "tidal motion" of his friend's blood (line 14). The cries of the poet

will have to descend to an Underworld to find these latter (lines 12–13). The words he seeks have sometimes seemed like a household of servants lingering unhelpfully behind his lips (line 3); then again, once they were serfs and now, freed, are difficult to control, making for what may be unbidden utterances in the mouths of prophets and the blind (lines 5–8).

L.3 *Ingesinde* "household" — Collective noun; the household servants of a large domestic establishment in former times.

L.11 *Sie gehn und kommen mit Gelegenheiten* "Which go and come as well they please" — Literally, "they go and come according to circumstance."

L.12 *alle Tage lang* "forever" — Literally, "through all the days." Here and in the following line Benjamin echoes the last stanza of Hölderlin's "Hyperions Schicksaalslied" and its famous image of mankind flung helplessly from one hour to the next "like water flung down from ledge to ledge for long years into the Unknown."

[60]   Taken altogether, the third and last group of Heinle sonnets (nos. 60–73) has more in common with the main group (nos. 1–50) than with the middle one (nos. 51–59). This is true both with regard to poetic technique and subject matter. However, nos. 60, 72, and 73 would seem to belong more with the sonnets of the second or middle group. Like these, they do not use his otherwise prevailing rhyme scheme (in the quatrains, of *abba baab*); are of smooth facture; and do not depend on brooding metaphysical and religious conceits. (Sonnet 72 may not even belong to the Heinle sphere at all.)

L.1 Literally: "If nights thou shouldst inspire me with a song of [for] thyself."

L.6 *Früchtegleich* "like ripe fruit" — Literally, "like fruits."

L.9 *Ihrer keines mehr* "Such fruit...no more" — The literal reference goes back to "words" (line 3) and a correspondingly literal translation would be: "no more of them" (of the words). But these words were compared to fruits (line 6) and here they hang enticingly from branches.

L.11 *unerschöpfliches* "endless unwearying" — Literally, "inexhaustible."

L.12 *Faßt* "grasps" (line 14) — The word has both a literal, physical sense and a figurative, intellectual one. It is worth noting that Hölderlin exploits this same double sense in the stanza from *Patmos* which Benjamin chose as the epigraph for his collection of sonnets (see lines 5–8, lines 5–7 in the English translation).

[61]

L.1–2 The New Testament (I Corinthians 15: 51–53) tells us that at the sound of the final trumpet the dead will be "raised imperishable" in an instant and shall put on an incorruptible nature. Here the dead are to be dressed in a "secret [hidden, mystical] Sound," equally "without decay [imperishable, incorruptible]."

L.3 *unverlierbar Name* "Inalienable Name" — See below, note for line 14; *sie* "they" — The dead, who find themselves "in thee," i.e., the secret Sound apostrophized by the poet.

L.5 *Wehr* "stronghold" — Literally, "defense." A rampart, keep, weapon, or body of armed men; *die sich keinem verschreibt* "which does yield to none" — Literally, "which makes itself over [by written deed] to none."

L.9 *die Schönen* "the Beautiful" — Persons possessing beauty, moral and physical, among them the poet's deceased friend.

L.11 *dein Widerschein* "thy second shining" — Literally, "thy reflection," i.e., a reflection of the "secret Sound." As a reflection, the Name of the friend shines for those who grieve. *Widerschein* extends the range of ideas Benjamin associates with *Schein*, a key term in his philosophy of beauty.

L.12 *die Dinge* "plain things" — Literally, "things," in the sense of things of everyday experience.

L.13 *Geheimere* "more secret ones" — The odd comparative substantive form of the adjective "geheim," which can mean "private," "secret," "concealed," or "occult."

L.14 *Erhabner Name* "Exalted Name" — The poet addresses not his friend but rather his friend's Name — one kept secret, not his given Christian name ("O secret sound," line 1). Through this mystical Name, beyond time and incorruptible, the poet seeks ultimate communion with the friend; whereas those memories which the poet keeps of the friend and their life together are an impediment to communion (lines 5–8). Still, the poet resorts to images when invoking the exalted Name itself—and at last in seeming resignation refers to it as the "stiff costume of the dead" (line 14).

[62]
    L.3 *Der große Schmerz* "Pain of pain"—Literally, "Great Hurt," pain personified. The theme of returning pain recalls sonnets 54 and 57.
    L.5 Literally: "So that all the chambers of the heart are flung open." Or possibly: "So that with all thy heart the chambers are flung open."
    L.13–14 Grammatically, "thy motion" would seem to refer unmistakably to the poet's own heart, which he has been addressing familiarly throughout the sonnet, and yet this makes his thought turn back on itself strangely. For a more logical outcome, the final "and" may be ignored so that "sounding" refers to "god's song" rather than to "vessel." Or: for "thy motion" read "its motion" (referring to "a god's song").

[63]   The poet means to compare his deceased friend with Jesus of Nazareth. He praises him as a prince of peace (lines 1–2) and like Jesus, the friend has had disciples and gone away from them (line 7). The poet says that he has become the recorder of the deeds of his departed friend (line 14), and we are reminded of those who produced the Gospels. The sonnet hints at activities of vast import which are left unexplained. Benjamin's account of the idealistic political work of Fritz Heinle and himself among Berlin university and high school students before the outbreak of war is preserved in the *Berlin Chronicle* (notices 12 and 13).
    L.4 *hienieden* "among us"—Literally, "here below."
    L.9–10 *vergangen das Land* "melted into air the land"—Literally, "vanished [diminished, wasted away, faded, melted] the land."
    L.11 *verloren was du angefangen* "fruitless all by thee begun"—Literally, "failed [for nought] what thou hast begun"
    L.12 *das Werben* "the wooing"—Can also mean "the recruiting [of soldiers]."

[64]   This sonnet is not without its mysteries. Still, when we hear that "Youth did crown itself with death" (line 1), it can only refer to the heroic action of Fritz

Heinle and Rika Seligson. But the identity of the swan who flies through its second quatrain and both of the tercets, as well as that of the dreaming sleeper (line 11) pose more of a puzzle. The latter, who looks to the former for his rescue, may be the sonnet writer. And swans, according to medieval legend, are rescuers in that they draw the skiff of mysterious knights intent on saving damsels in distress. (They are anyway ubiquitous in late-Romantic and Jugendstil art and literature.) Benjamin's swan is a pupil of the Day, perhaps best understood as supernatural light, or even life eternal. Wherever this swan flies it scatters light, and its goal is a dew-besprinkled hill awaiting the dawn (see also Sonnet 19).

L.3 *späte* "belated" — Can also mean "late"; *legt...an* "makes landing" — Has the specific meaning of "lays anchor."

L.5 *der große Schwann* "the great-spanned swan" —Literally, "the big [large] swan."

L.12 *nachtbesonnten* "sunning in the night" — A nonce-word; literally, "receiving sun by night."

L.12–14 Benjamin's oddly sprung syntax cannot be reproduced in translation.

L.14 *zum Hügel den der Tau besprengte* "to the hill made bright with dew" — Literally, "towards the hill which the dew sprinkled."

[65]   The pair of butterflies who tire soaring in the blue may be Fritz Heinle and Rika Seligson, or a figure for them. The Soul which flew into the land of shadows (line 4) belongs to the poet's friend, and now Remembering — the poet's memories of him — seeks that Soul in death as a mate (line 6). The poet's image of the friend shall remain as long as "above the altar tears still burn" (line 8). But images are vain; both the friend's gaze (line 9) and his words (line 11) are now denied the poet, and the far-off thunder of a slowly moving storm furnishes him with an image of his friend's vanished speech. Any glimpse of his friend's Soul, "which flees Remembering" (lines 12–13), will come to him as an image that Nature "draws down" (like rain) from the sky (line 14) — and will prove insufficient in the way all images do.

L.3 *Thymian* "thyme" — The ancient Greeks made the plant a symbol of courage and sacrifice. Here is one clue to the identity of the pair of butterflies.

L.5 *Gemüt* "Heart" — Can also mean "Soul."

L.6 *Das Erinnern* "Remembering" — The poet's remembering, personified.

L.6 *den treuen Gatten* "the faithful spouse" — Literally, "the faithful [true, loyal] husband."

L.8 *Wo* "While" — Literally, "where."

L.12 Literally: "And for their [the words'] shower [it] distantly delays and thunders [rumbles]"

L.13–14 A free rendering of the two concluding lines, which are somewhat ambiguous. An alternative reading for the last line: "Nature alone draws down an image."

[66]   Once again, as in sonnets 5 and 21, the voice of the poet's dead friend is paramount. Whereas in no. 5 it is experienced as transcendently remote, beyond the ken of the grieving poet, here the poet waits to hear the voice and vows to obey its commands. The present sonnet offers a contrast with Sonnet 21, too; there the friend's voice is heard in an ominous dream and seems to compel the poet to follow in its wake.

L.1–3 When he heard "this call" before, the poet did not follow it. The self-critical implication allies this sonnet with nos. 13 and 39.

L.3 *seine Stimme* "his voice" — In reference to the poet's deceased friend. Less plausible would be the rendering "its voice" (referring to "this call," line 1).

L.5 *jene Stimme die da will* "that voice which wants me there" — Seemingly an abbreviated construction, not clear in meaning. The translator has supplied an object as though the line read: "jene Stimme die mich da will."

L.6 *dessen was wir leiden* "[of] what we tolerate" — Can also be rendered with: "of what we suffer from."

L.11–12 A memory of the words once uttered by the deceased friend seems to escape from the hands of the poet, who will then pursue it even to the "seat of God."

L.13 *als deinen Folger* "As thy follower" — Clearly an allusion to the poet's friend, who once again is presented as a Christ-like figure with disciples.

254

[67]

L.3 *unser Leben* "our life" — The lives of the poet and others left behind.

L.5 Although there has been no mention of "hours" (*Stunden*), the word must be supplied. The whole of the second quatrain will concern those hours the poet spends waiting for a new communion with the departed ones.

L.6 Literally: "In the lethargic hourglass the remainder of sand is running off [dwindling]."

L.8 *uns die fast erstarrten* "we who were grown nearly numb" — Numb, that is, with cold.

L.9 *uns ... die wir harrten* "us waiting ones" —Literally, "we who were [intently, longingly] waiting." A messianic sentiment.

L.10 *Aus Euren Lebens* "of your life" — An unmistakable allusion to Fritz Heinle and Rika Seligson.

L.13 *im Gedächtnis* " in mind" — That is, in the memories of those left behind.

[68]

L.1 *sein Tod* "his death" — An unmediated reference to Benjamin's friend, Fritz Heinle. The sonnet seems to trace his agonies as he (actually, his Soul) is contemplating suicide.

L.2 *Purpurnen Baum* "a crimson tree" (lines 1–2) —Literally, "like a crimson tree."

L.7 *Dem herrischen Gefallen* "to the lordly pleasure" — Death as Lord may ask whatever he wishes of the Soul.

L.11 *Den Lethebecher schlürft* "She sips from Lethe's goblet" — An allusion to suicide.

L.13 *Der Seele* "for her" — Here a pronoun referring to "the Soul" would seem preferable to Benjamin's restatement of the noun.

L.14 Literally: "The simpleness [innocence, foolishness] of those refusing lives without delay" — A reference to Fritz Heinle and Rika Seligson and to their simple refusal to go on living once war had been declared in August 1914. Now they live in eternity, in the simplicity of moral greatness.

[69]

L.4 *dem letzten Land* "to the final land" — A reference to the longed-for existence after death.

L.9 *Der ewge Reigen* "Everlasting dancers" — Literally, "the everlasting party of dancers."

L.10 *Geschwister* "siblings" — Literally, "brother(s) and sister(s)." In the afterlife, there will be no sexual interest as we know it; all will be as brothers and sisters to one another. Several other sonnets invoke sisters or sisterliness to suggest chasteness or modesty (see nos. 31, 46, and 73).

L.12 *ein Schein* "shining" — See the note to Sonnet 10, line 14.

L.13 *ihren* "their" — A problematic pronoun. The German does not allow us to refer "their senses" back to the "everlasting dancers" — though doing so makes sense of the sonnet.

L.14 *Amarant* "amaranth" — An imaginary flower which does not fade.

[70]   Benjamin's herald announces the end of ordinary time. Eternity and the moment ("the hour") are the same to him (line 3). Each thing shaped by time will usher in its opposite: If pains are to heal, then old wounds already closed will open (lines 5 and 8). Perhaps the "unseen host" which follows this herald (line 11) are all those who have ever died. Invisible to us, they could be present in the timeless air being announced, even as the herald empties land and sky before him of visible things (lines 9–10). His song ("Lied," line 9) has a corresponding sorrow ("Leid," line 12) as manyheaded as the grass; hearing the song, this sorrow wakens to hush a mysterious crying that may represent all crying.

L.2 *die Runde* "the vault" — That is, the vault of heaven; the sky.

L.8 *eure* "your" — Benjamin has not capitalized the second-person plural pronoun as he does in all other sonnets where such references point to Fritz Heinle and Rika Seligson.

L.10 Literally: "Clouds flee before such a trumpeter as this."

L.14 *das Weinen* "the crying" — An impersonal construction in German.

256

[71]   The sonnet concerns itself with the tremendous presence of the deceased friend's mystical Name (see also sonnets 1 and 61) in the life of the poet and the others left behind. This presence is compared with the coming of Judgment Day and its terrors (lines 9–12). The Name reveals, as will Judgment Day itself, the utter darkness in which we are living on earth. The last two lines of the sonnet suggest that the friend's Name is immeasurable — that it is an infinity which keeps silent and forgets. These lines remind us of the "expressionless" condition of the friend as set forth in Sonnet 10. Meditating on the friend's Name, the poet seeks to approach the pure Being of messianic time, or ultimate reality (which is satisfied to exist within and for itself, giving no sign of itself and silently forgetting all else.)

   L.2 *seinen Namen* "that Name of his" — A reference to the deceased friend and his mystical Name.

   L.2 *welcher heimberuft* "which calls us home" — In the Christian sense of calling [a person] home to eternal life.

   L.5 *ihm* "it" — Referring to "that Name of his."

   L.5 *Gruft* "vault" (line 7) — Tomb, burial vault, mausoleum.

   L.7 *der Auferstehenden* "of ones about to rise again" (line 6) — In the Christian sense of those who shall rise from the dead.

   L.8 Literally: "If the heavenly one should one day blow [the trumpet] out from pure air."

   L.13 *ihn* "it" — The reference is ultimately ambiguous, and may be to "Evening" (line 11) as much as to "his Name" (line 9).

[72]   How this dream-sonnet with run-on imagery leading to the discovery of the (sculpted) body of a dazzling woman might fit in a collection of Heinle sonnets remains uncertain. Perhaps its second line ("Luckless and yet freed of my old sorrow") offers the clue.

   L.4 *Verlarvter* "shrouded" — Literally, "disguised" or "masked."

   L.11 *Schwermut* "sorrow" — Literally, "melancholy" or "despondency."

   L.12 *weite* "flowing" — Literally, "wide," "broad," or "loosely fitting [clothing]."

   L.13 *blendendsten* "blindingest" — The most dazzling of women, and perhaps the most deceiving.

[73]   The last sonnet of the third group of Heinle sonnets most resembles the first sonnet of the intermediate group (no. 51). In both the poet shows himself self-consciously going about the business of writing sonnets. Moreover, these two sonnets exhibit a similar high finish and unruffled composure which are in keeping with their Greek settings. No such distanced and thoroughly "pagan" poems are found in Benjamin's principal set of fifty (sonnets 1–50).

L.6 *eingehegten* "penned-up" — Literally, "fenced-in."

L.8 *Opfer* "gift" — Literally, "offering" or "sacrifice."

L.9 *wo die Worte sich ... ranken* "where words ... clamber up" — A complex image. Most often it is grapevines that clamber up lattices. Here, though, it is "words" — those of the sonnet — and they "clamber up" the sonnet itself, made of lines and resembling a ladder. As the poet pens this sonnet, words clamber up and inspire him as would wine (and yet they climb "like sisters"; see Sonnet 69, note for line 10).

L.14 *seine Statt* "his grave" — Usually *Statt* is the equivalent of *Stätte*, and means simply "place"; in elevated discourse it implies a place reserved for a certain purpose. Such a place is the friend's grave or sepulcher (*Grabstätte*). By means of untranslatable wordplay the German makes us see the poet place his mouth directly upon the grave of his friend.

There are very few concrete references in Benjamin's sonnets. One of these would be to the grave of Fritz Heinle's companion, Rika Seligson (see Sonnet 47). Records at the Weissensee Friedhof, where 115,000 persons have been buried, indicate that she lies in "zone L4, first row," but no stone remains for her there. Why a stone is missing is not known; the above photo shows the immediate vicinity of her grave. This portion of the Weissensee cemetery, the largest Jewish burial ground in Europe, has not been well maintained (many other areas have been restored). Where Fritz Heinle, Seligson's lover, was buried no one knows (see Sonnet 40).

nimmer er zu sterben

Er könnte ja auch weiter leben (er hätte ja auch zu den
(verwundet zurück(?)) fliegen gemeldet), aber der Aspekte des Kampfes wäre
jetzt vorbei, jetzt noch weiter zu leben wäre sinnlos.
Diese Haltung sei die heroischste.
Seine ersten Gedichte wären zwar im Innerste sehr ernst, wären
aber unwahr.

Er hätte auch gebetet darum, daß er nicht zu sterben
brauche, aber es ginge nicht, er würde sterben.
Er sei — wie sein Bruder eine Blüte, auf die der Frost
gefallen ist. Er hat soll Gedanken zu Ende gedacht
er sollte nicht auf einen andern Stege erwandern können. Aber
diese Religion ...

Nun geht seit dem Todestage seines Bruders, würde
faßte wieder neue Pläne für sein Gluck, allerend
anderend etwas besser, ist aber, vermutlich (will ein Bild
durch das Mädchen, das er jetzt in mit sein
Bruder gewinn herzogen)
Nikkersdorf besucht hat, wieder
besonders dringend geworden. Seine Angehörige, Benjamin u
Frau Behrendt, unterstützen ihn indirekt dadurch daß sie
„Ernstlich gewinnen" haben, eine Geste gut steigen und
die „Verantwortung nicht übernehmen können" es sich zu überleg
und ihn in seiner „Vollendung" zu stören. Das Bild
dem sie mit ihm treiben, steigert seinen Willen zu diese

A page of the "Loewenson MS."

APPENDICES

I. THE LOEWENSON DOCUMENT

Address
Wolf Heinle
Grunewald
Berlin
Sanatorium Grunewald
von Helene Mayer
Hagenstr. 45

FRITZ HEINLE and Erika Seligson fatally poisoned with lighting gas ca. 9 Aug., kitchen of the Soziales Amt. According to the newspaper: because of love troubles. According to Wolf Heinle: because of the war.

Wolf Heinle, who was very close to his brother especially of late, wants to kill himself

1) because of his despair over the war and because he foresees the general demise of the Spiritual [*den Untergang des Geistigen*]; and then also, in addition: "Love is everything, through the death of his brother the source of love has been taken from him."

His thoughts: He says that he wants to die like Christ, so as to be always there for a group of persons (when Christ left [?] the world, he created a group of persons); and that only through his death can he truly exist for these persons, since he already feels himself growing worse now. One must either have the spirit of youth [*jugendlich sein*] or be dead.

If he had been the right sort of child, the war could not have happened. Of course he, Wolf, cannot blame the world for this now, but the Spirit which comes from Heaven. Therefore one ought not reflect on things logically, one must instead feel them. Death is not destruction, *but a fulfillment*. It is his duty to die — His brother is leading a life of light. After death we shall meet again. Spiritual persons cannot live through wars. All wonderful things are now being destroyed. After this will come a more stupid nationalism.

And besides, there is a girl [*Mädl*] who means as much to him as Rika did to Fritz. In order to show these two great honor, he too must die.

He could indeed go on living (he would have joined the airmen), but the most extreme part of the struggle is now behind him, to go on living now would be shameful. He thinks this attitude is the most heroic. He says his first poems were truly very serious in their inmost nature, but they were untrue.

Yes, he had prayed that there was no need for him to die, but this did not work, he must die. He is — like his brother — a flower on which the frost has fallen. He, Fritz, only thought ideas out to the end. He, Wolf, will arrive at the very same place by another path. By way of his religion . . .

This has been going on since the day his brother died, at first he seemed to be getting better (he made new plans for his future, worked on poems also the literary remains he wants to issue a book with his brother), but apparently through the girl whom he has now visited in Wickersdorf he has gotten really bad again. His milieu, Benjamin and Suse Behrendt, give him indirect support when they say they have "gained the insight" and call his gesture good, and that they "cannot assume responsibility to think over things" [*die Verantwörtung nicht übernehmen können . . . es sich zu überlegen*] and to disturb him in "his fulfillment" [*in seiner Vollendung*]. The cult [*Cult*] which they promote with him strengthens his will to this deed insofar as he sees himself reflected in their adoration [*Anbetung*] and feels himself half obliged for their sake to carry it out. If he could be isolated from these two, that would already be a very good thing; their influence over him must be broken by Jentzsch. Gutmann and Loewenson, who have tried to dissuade him from this decision, each separately, are finished for him, after a quick discussion.

Jentzsch wanted to write him a letter at once, *but he must learn nothing of all this*. Because of the extraordinary danger and the importance of the man, *this will be entrusted to him only if he exercises discretion* (the things Koffka has collected on this point); and indeed under the pretense of wanting to know about the deaths of Fritz and Rika and to offer his "condolences," and because he might reasonably fear that the same thing might happen to Wolf. First — since it is very quick and will arrive on the same day, let him dispatch a telegram to Wolf saying something like "have just learned of Fritz Heinle's death, letter tomorrow" and then *immediately* he should write him a detailed letter which should work to free him of the train of thoughts previously mentioned (especially the ones which come from Christianity). But Jentzsch ought to write only if he really is able to say something very forcefully and without qualification against *this* suicide (Wolf's). If he is able only to agree with his despair, his decision, and his view of religion (*casting off this life allows one to enter into a better one*), then he should not express any opinion whatsoever. (It is very important to be completely *dictatorial* when writing Robert Jentzsch).

There remains the possibility of perhaps having him influenced through George (Even though he has said that he is *more* than George). J. could on this account write to Koffka, to see if perhaps he can furnish a connection through the Georgians, who are in Munich at the moment. Perhaps provide addresses of Georgians in Berlin.

The energy (and the lust for domination [*Herrschsucht*] which has come about through the cult) is now being used by Wolf to fortify his desire to die [*Wollust zu sterben*]. The milieu (now only Benjamin and Suse Behrendt, at first there was still Willi Caro, a schoolboy, and Traute Seligson, a sister of the deceased) is completely under his influence and has borrowed his same gestures, his same smile (that of being above it all) and his same body movements. (The influence of Loewenson and Guttmann should be reinforced for now.) Please formulate all this in your own way and do not include this note with your letter.

Thanks so very much. Wolf's address on the 1ˢᵗ page.

Note: This MS is preserved among the papers of Erwin Loewenson in the Deutsches Literaturarchiv, Marbach, under the rubric "Protokoll vom August 1914" (68.1052). The writer's identity is confirmed by an annotation in the left margin of the first page: "Bin um 12 Uhr unten Loewenson," which is in the same hand as that used for the body of the MS. The persons named in the MS are briefly identified in Steizinger (*Revolte, Eros und Sprache*).

II. OTHER SONNETS BY WALTER BENJAMIN

Seven sonnets survive which were addressed by Benjamin to women. One of them was written for his wife, Dora; five were destined for Jula Cohn, with whom Benjamin was passionately in love in 1921; and a final sonnet is associated with a Dutch woman, Annemarie (Toet) Blaupot ten Cate, whom Benjamin met on the island of Ibiza in 1933. Though the majority of these sonnets share in the elevated tone of Benjamin's Heinle sonnets, they are all contingent upon situations borne of ongoing relationships. They are true occasional poems and exhibit momentary flashes of a lover's (even a husband's) irony and wit.

The sonnet for Dora Benjamin, dated January 6, 1922, appears to represent an effort on the part of Walter Benjamin to reconcile with her by appealing to the shared love of their only son. In the late sonnet for Blaupot ten Cate ("for [B.]"), the poet pleads with his beloved not to withdraw from his presence. The five sonnets for Jula Cohn, all likely written during the summer of 1921 when Benjamin's infatuation for her was at its peak, let us glimpse an anxious (and impecunious) wooer unsure of his lover and yet alive to romantic possibilities.

I. Zum 6ten Januar 1922

Wie heißt der Gast daß ob er auch versehrt
Der Herrin Haus und Trübsal ihr beschert
Sich dessen Pforte dennoch so geschwind
Ihm auftut wie ein leichtes Tor dem Wind?

Sein Nam ist Zwietracht welche wiederkehrt
Wiewohl sie Tisch und Kammern längst geleert
Der Seele bleibt ihr dreifach Ingesind
Nun einzig treu: Schlaf Tränen und das Kind[1]

Doch jeden Tages schwerterblanke Garbe
Schlägt der Erwachenden die alte Narbe
Und eh sie Trost in neuen Schlummer wiegt

Ist ihr der Quell der Tränen längst versiegt
Allein des Kindes Lächeln seine Sitten
Vermögen Hoffnung in ihr Haus zu bitten.

I. For January 6, 1922

And for which guest though he lay waste
The mistress's house and leave her in distress
Will yet its portals swing as quickly wide
As does a flimsy gate before the wind?

His name is Discord who returns e'en though
She's long since cleared both table and the rooms
Now of the Soul these matchless servants three
Shall by her stand: sleep tears and the child[1]

Still each day's exchange between swords drawn
But strikes the waking one's old scars
And ere she's rocked by Consolation to

New slumber is her spring of tears run dry
Alone the smiling of the child his ways
Can bid Hope welcome to her house.

---

1   *das Kind* "the child" — Stefan Rafael Benjamin (1918–72) would have been three months short of his fourth birthday when the sonnet was written. Any reconciliation achieved by his parents at this time was temporary. From 1923 on Walter and Dora Benjamin lived under one roof but no longer as man and wife. They divorced in 1930.

II. In trüben Gedanken

Was ich erwogen will sich nun vollenden[1]
Und wolle Gott es sei noch nicht zu spät
Daß die verhohlne Hoffnung mir gerät
So bring ich sie mit allen ihren Bränden

Vor dich: die Angst   Auf meines Herzens Händen
Sie sind mit Schrund und Narben übersät
Hätt ich so lange nach dir ausgespät
Wenn sie nicht dennoch in die deinen fänden?

Du aber wisse mich bereit zum Tausch
Dem mächtigen der jeder Angst gebot:
Ich suche die Genesung und den Rausch

Drum nehme ich aus deiner Hand die Not
Damit das Leben das wir beide teilen[2]
Bewogen sei hienieden zu verweilen.

II. When I have Dark Thoughts

What I pondered shall now come to pass[1]
And please God that it be not yet too late
For Hope unspoken to turn out well for me
With all her flarings I will offer her

To you: Anxiety   On my heart's hands
Oversewn are they with chaps and scars
Though had I looked for you so long
Were they not to find a passage into yours?

Know that I am ready to exchange me for
The strong man who has mastered each anxiety:
I seek healing and exhiliration

And therefore take affliction from your hand
So that this life which we both share[2]
May be disposed to linger here below.

---

1   *Was ich erwogen will sich nun vollenden* "What I pondered shall now come to pass" —
Possibly the reference is to an imminent meeting.

2   *Damit das Leben...bewogen sei...zu verweilen* "So that this life...may be disposed to lin-
ger" The poet seems to be hinting that one or even both parties had been entertaining thoughts
of suicide.

III. Vergängnis[1]

Daß du vor andern die Gestalt verehrt[2]
Die du vor andern schön bist ist mir kund
Und dennoch höre es durch meinen Mund[3]
Was uns der Abend da wir schieden lehrt

Am Horizont versank das volle Rund
Von dem wir uns verweilend abgekehrt
Dann traf mein Blick von deinem nah beschwert
Den unermeßlich goldnen Himmelsgrund

Der Glast der Sonne hatte sich verloren
Verwobnes Licht erfüllte ihn noch lange
Da habe ich dein Bild in mir beschworen

Und sieh es stand in ewigem Untergange
Und flammte aus den tausend stumpfen Gluten
Der Augen der noch eben auf mich ruhten.

III. Pastness[1]

That you have honored Form[2] more than the others
Who than the others are more beautiful I know
And yet prepare to hear it from my mouth[3]
What the evening when we parted teaches

Horizonward the round of heaven sank
From which we only slowly turned away
So did my gaze weighed down by yours close by
Encounter endless golden depths on high

Vanished was the brightness of the sun
The warp and woof of light still filling them
Then your image I did conjure in myself

And lo it stood declining now and always
And flamed out of the thousand dim dull fires
Of those eyes which were yet resting on me.

---

1   Title: See the note for line 1 of Sonnet 20.

2   *Dass du . . . die Gestalt verehrt* "That you have honored Form" — Jula Cohn was a sculptor.

3   *Und dennoch höre es durch meinem Mund* "And yet prepare to hear it from my mouth" — Though his sculptor-friend reveres Form "more than the others," the poet will dare to give form to his sentiments through this sonnet.

IV. Zu den vorigen ein neues

Nicht arm vor dich zu treten[1] — so bescheiden
So reich vor deinem Blicke zu bestehn
Das wollten jene Jahren sich erflehn
In denen Sehnsucht vorgab dich zu meiden

Muß ich tagtäglich herrlicher dich sehn —
Mich soll Entfernung um so schöner kleiden
Ins Wort der Liebe darf ich als in seiden-
Und goldene Gewandung übergehn

Doch Schönheit kennt Genüge — nicht die Lust[2]
Die ich an dir mit tausend Fibern[3] nehme
Lied quillt und Träne aus deselben Brust

Die ihrer Fülle sich als Mangel schäme
Und schließt das Lied[4] — die Fülle der Sonette
Befriediget kein Kranz und keine Kette.

IV. Another to Add to the Others

Not to stand before you poor[1] — demure
And no less rich to last before your look
Is what those years imploring sought to gain
In which desire did pretend to shun you

Must I see you each day more exquisite —
Then let distance clothe me all the finer
So may I slip into the words of love
As were they gowns of silk and gold

Still beauty may be sating — not the pleasure[2]
That I take in you through countless fibers[3]
Song and tears are springing from one breast

Which feels its fullness as a shaming lack
And should song stop[4] — nor crown nor chain
Suffices for the fullness of my sonnets.

---

1   *Nicht arm vor dich zu treten* "Not to stand before you poor" — Benjamin had fallen into impoverished circumstances after his parents ceased to support him and his family.

2   *Lust* "pleasure" — Powerfully sensual pleasure or joy is meant.

3   *Mit tausend Fibern* "Through countless fibers." — Literally, "with a thousand fibers."

4   *Und schließt das Lied…* "And should song stop…" — Perhaps the "stop" here is a literal one, so that the remainder of these lines becomes its own complete thought: "No crown or chain of sonnets is enough to express what I want to express in them."

V. Sonett in der Nacht

Andere Nacht du der Liebe Verlassenheit[1]
Welche der Einsame stets zu vertauschen sich sehnt
Mit jener flüchtigeren die Erfüllung verleiht
Du auch mit dem Licht eines Sternes belehnt

Liebenden bleibt er vor Venus immer geweiht
Wenn sich das tröstlose Herz nach dem tröstenden dehnt
Ziehet der Mächtige[2] auf der die schwindende Zeit
Wachsend ihnen ermißt nach Jahr und Jahrzehnt

Und er strahlte auch mir aus trüben verfinsterndem Grame
Aber der Liebenden Mond der Geliebtesten Name
Nimmer wollte der goldene dennoch sich runden

Wenn er sein milderes Licht in unzähligen Stunden
Auf mein Antlitz geworfen doch über ein Kleines[3]
Strahlet ihn Jula das deinige voller in meines.

V. Sonnet in the Night

O fresh night of love abandoned[1]
Which the lonely one does ever yearn to change
For some more fleeting night of love fulfilled
As well are you enfeoffed with light whose star

Is always bound to lovers even before Venus
When unconsoled the heart swells towards consoling heart
The Mighty One[2] will rise and waxing measure
For them time's decay by year and by years ten

And for me too it shone forth from the dim eclipse of grief
Though still the lovers' moon the name of those most loved
The golden one would never let itself grow round

All during hours numberless it cast a milder light
Upon my face and yet in but a little while[3]
Yours Jula will shine it into mine more fully.

---

1   Literally: "Another night you the abandonment of love."

2   *der Mächtige* "The Mighty One" — The moon.

3   *über ein Kleines* "in but a little while" — The words of Jesus' promise made to his disciples in John 14:19 (Luther Bible): "Yet a little while, and the world will see me no more, but you will see me...."

VI. Erweckung

Du schliefest in der Gemme[1] eine Braut
Vor irdischen Begegnungen gefeit
Und wahrtest einen Atem Ewigkeit
In deinem Busen den kein Kuß betaut

Dich Weiberschaffen die als Gott gebaut
Hielt Lust in Banden schon fürs Grab bereit
In tausend Händen dennoch unentweiht
Uraltes Erbstück bist du mir vertraut

Wenn ich im Lied so tiefen Schlummer störe
Geschieht es nur weil ich dir bessern spende
Den süßen Schlaf Lebendiger der am Ende

Der Nächte ist die ich für uns beschwöre
In welchen die Berührung ihrer Hände
Den Ruhenden sich kund tut wie zwei Chöre.

VI. Awakening

Within the gem you slept[1] a bride
Made safe from earth's encounters
And of eternity did guard a breath
Within your breast which no kiss may bedew

O womanly form in keeping with God's make
Desire held you bound and ready for the grave
And yet unstained from endless hands you
Came into my keeping as an heirloom out of time

If I disturb in song a slumber so profound
My one excuse is that I send to you a
Better: sweet sleep of the living from

The end of nights which I invoke for us
Wherein the touching of their hands proclaims
Itself to those at rest as do two choirs.

---

1   *Du schliefest in der Gemme* "Within the gem you slept"— Sonnet 25 also introduces an image held by a carved gem. Here the poet wishes to waken the passions of his friend, whom he compares to an image kept intact ("sleeping," "unstained from endless hands") within semi-precious stone.

VII. An [B.]

dein wort ist für die dauer wie dein leib
dein atem schmeckt nach stein und nach metall[1]
dein blick rollt mir entgegen wie ein ball
das schweigen ist dein bester zeitvertreib

wie war dem ersten mann das erste weib[2]
so standest du vor mir und überall
trifft dich nun meiner bitte wiederhall
der tausend zungen hat. sie lautet: bleib

du bist die ungerufene unbekannte
und wohnst in mir im herzen einer stille
in die dich weder traum noch sehnsucht bannte[3]

nichts mehr bewirken vorsatz oder wille
seitdem der erste blick in dir erkannte
die doppel herrin: hure und sybille.

To [B.]

for lasting is your word just like your body
your breath tastes both of stone and metal[1]
your look rolls towards me like a ball
and keeping silent is your finest hobby

as was first Eve for first Adam[2]
so you stood before me and in all places
you are met now with the echo of my plea
which has a thousand tongues. namely: stay

you are she unsummoned she unknown
and live in me within a heart of stillness
into which no dream no yearning banned you[3]

nothing can be done by purpose or my will
since that first look did see in you
the double mistress: whore and sybil.

---

1   *dein atem schmeckt nach stein und nach metall* "your breath tastes both of stone and metal" — Only in this late sonnet are there obvious suggestions of a physically consummated affair.

2   Literally: "As was the first woman for the first man."

3   Can also be read as: "Into which no dream no yearning bewitched you."

BIBLIOGRAPHY

Adorno, Theodor W. *Über Walter Benjamin* [Concerning Walter Benjamin]. Rolf Tiedemann, ed. Frankfurt am Main: Suhrkamp Verlag, 1970.

Baudelaire, Charles. *Tableaux parisiens. Deutsche Übertragung mit einem Vorwort über die Aufgabe des Übersetzers von Walter Benjamin* ["Tableaux parisiens." German Translation with a Foreword Concerning the Duty of the Translator, by Walter Benjamin]. Heidelberg: Verlag von Richard Weißbach, 1923. Die Drucke des Argonautenkreises 5

Belmore, Herbert W. "Walter Benjamin." German Life and Letters, new series, XV/4 (1962), pp. 309–313.

Benjamin, Walter. Berliner *Kindheit um* 1900. Trans. and with commentary and afterword by Carl Skoggard as Berlin Childhood ca. 1900. Portland, Ore.: Publication Studio, 2010.

Benjamin, Walter. *Berliner Chronik*. Trans. and with commentary by Carl Skoggard as The "Berlin Chronicle" Notices. Portland, Ore.: Publication Studio, 2011.

Benjamin, Walter. *Briefe* [Letters]. 2 vols.; ed. and annotated by Gershom Scholem and Theodor W. Adorno. 2nd ed.; Frankfurt am Main: Suhrkamp Verlag, 1993. Trans. by Manfred R. Jacobson and issued in English as The Correspondence of Walter Benjamin, U. of Chicago Press, 1994.

Benjamin, Walter. *Gesammelte Briefe* [Collected Letters]. 6 vols.; ed. and annotated by Christoph Gödde and Henri Lonitz. Frankfurt am Main: Suhrkamp Verlag, 1995–2000.

Benjamin, Walter. *Illuminations*. Ed. and with introduction by Hannah Arendt; essays trans. by Harry Zohn; preface by Leon Wieseltier. New York: Schocken Books, 2007 [reprint edition; originally issued in 1968 by Harcourt, Brace & World].

Benjamin, Walter. *Sonette* [Sonnets]. Ed. and with an afterword by Rolf Tiedemann. Frankfurt am Main: Suhrkamp Verlag, 1986. Includes an appendix: "Documentation on Benjamin and Heinle."

Benjamin, Walter. *Sonetti e poesie sparse* [Sonnets and Miscellaneous Poems]. Ed. and with an afterword by Rolf Tiedemann. Milan: Guilio Einaudi, 2010. A bilingual German-Italian edition of Benjamin's sonnets and his other poems [various translators].

Boie, Bernhild. "Dichtung als Ritual der Erlösung. Zu den wiedergefundenen Sonetten von Walter Benjamin." [Poetry as a Ritual of Redemption. Concerning the Rediscovered Sonnets Written by Walter Benjamin.] Akzente XXXI/1, pp. 23–39.

Brocke, Michael. "'Freundschaft der fremden Freunde': Walter Benjamin zum 60. Todestag." [Friendship among Friends as Strangers: For the 60th Anniversary of Walter Benjamin's Death]. Beiträge zur deutsch-jüdischen Geschichte aus dem Salomon Ludwig Steinheim-Institut (2000) III, pp. 6–8.

Brodersen, Momme. *Klassenbild mit Walter Benjamin. Eine Spurensuche.* [Class Portrait with Walter Benjamin. A Search for Traces]. München: Siedler Verlag, 2012. Provides a biography for each member of Benjamin's graduating class, Kaiser-Friedrich-Schule, Berlin, 1912.

Brodersen, Momme. *Spinne im eigenen Netz: Walter Benjamin Leben und Werk.* [Spider in his Own Net: Walter Benjamin, Life and Work]. Bühl-Moos: Elster-Verlag, 1990.

Dudek, Peter. *Fetisch Jugend. Walter Benjamin und Siegfried Bernfeld — Jugendprotest am Vorabend des Ersten Weltkrieges* [Youth fetish. Walter Benjamin and Siegfried Bernfeld — Youth Protest on the Eve of the First World War].

Bad Heilbrunn: Verlag Julius Klinkhardt, 2002. A valuable survey of the German and Austrian "youth culture movement."

Eiland, Howard, and Michael W. Jennings, eds. *Walter Benjamin: A Critical Life.* Cambridge: Mass. and London: The Belknap Press of Harvard U. Press, 2014.

George, Stefan. *Shakespeare Sonnette: Umdichtung* [The Shakespeare Sonnets: A Recasting]. Berlin: Georg Bondi Verlag, 1909. Translations for all 154 sonnets retain Shakespeare's meter and his rhyme scheme(s).

Hellingrath, Norbert von. *Pindarübertragungen von Hölderlin: Prolegomena zu einer Erstausgabe.* Kunstcharacter der Hölderlinischen übertragungen und ihre stellung in der geschichte der Pindarverdeutschung [Pindar Translations by Hölderlin: Prolegomena to a First Edition. The Art-character of the Hölderlinian Translations and their Place in the History of Rendering Pindar into German]. Jena: Eugen Diederichs Verlag, 1911.

Kraft, Werner. *Herz und Geist: Gesammelte Aufsätze zur deutschen Literatur* [Heart and Mind: Collected Essays on German Literature]. Vienna and Cologne: Böhlau Verlag, 1989. Literatur und Leben, new series, vol. 35. Includes two chapters on Heinle.

Lindner, Burkhardt, ed. *Benjamin Handbuch: Leben— Werk—Wirkung* [The Benjamin Handbook: Life — Work — Impact]. Stuttgart und Weimar: Verlag J.B. Metzler, 2011. See in particular: "The Sonette an Heinle" [Die Sonnets to Heinle] by Reinhold Görling, pp. 585–591; and "Zwei Gedichte von Friedrich Hölderlin," by Patrick Primavesi, pp. 465–471.

McCole, John. *Walter Benjamin and the Antinomies of Tradition.* Ithaca and London: Cornell University Press, 1993. Chapter 1 is titled "Benjamin and the Idea of Youth."

Puttnies, Hans, and Gary Smith. *Benjaminiana.* Giessen: Anabas Verlag, 1991. Werkbund Archiv 22. See Chapter 1, "Privatissimum." Includes a photograph said to be of C. Friedrich Heinle, 1912.

Scholem, Gershom. *Tagebücher nebst Aüfsatze und Entwürfen bis 1923* [Diaries Together with Essays and Drafts, to 1923]. 2 vols.; Frankfurt am Main: Jüdischer Verlag, 1995.

Scholem, Gershom. *Walter Benjamin–die Geschichte einer Freundschaft* [The History of a Friendship]. Frankfurt am Main: Suhrkamp Verlag, 1990 [rev. ed.]. Original ed. trans. by Harry Zohn as Walter Benjamin: The Story of a Friendship (Philadelphia, 1981).

Steizinger, Johannes. *Revolte, Eros und Sprache. Walter Benjamins 'Metaphysik der Jugend'* [Revolt, Eros, and Language. Walter Benjamin's "Metaphysik der Jugend"]. PhD diss., U. Wien, 2012. Appendices include previously unpublished letters written to Benjamin by Carla Seligson in 1913 and 1914; all known poems by Heinle; and a transcript of the Erwin Loewenson MS.

Wipf, Hans-Ulrich. *Studentische Politik und Kulturreform: Geschichte der Freistudenten-Bewegung, 1896–1918* [Student Politics and Cultural Reform: The History of the Free Students Movement, 1896–1918]. Schwalbach am Taunus: Wochenschau Verlag, 2004.

Wizisla, Erdmut. Walter Benjamin. Friedrich Heinle. Ernst Joël. Weltanschauung, *Literatur und Politik in der Berliner Freien Studentenschaft 1912–1917* [Walter Benjamin. Friedrich Heinle. Ernst Joël. Weltanschauung, Literature, and Politics in the Freie Studentenschaft Berlin, 1912–1917]. Diplomarbeit, Humboldt-Universität zu Berlin, 1987.

Wyneken, Gustav. *Die Kampf für die Jugend. Gesammelte Aufsätze* [The Battle for Youth. Collected Essays]. Jena: Eugen Diederichs Verlag, 1920.

ACKNOWLEDGEMENTS

It is a great pleasure to take this opportunity to thank those persons who helped and encouraged me in this work. My very good friend Ursula Tax made many contributions. I would like most of all to thank her for systematically reviewing my translations during a series of long and fruitful discussions in Berlin in April of 2013. I am indebted to her for many excellent suggestions made then and later. I am also grateful for help I received from Dr. Sissi Tax, for her eagle-eyed review of my translations and commentary and more generally for giving me forthright encouragement to undertake the sonnets project in the first place. And then too: When I am in Berlin, I stay in her delightfully casual Charlottenburg apartment, where I am always made to feel at home.

The Walter Benjamin Archiv, Berlin, provided me with every assistance during two visits I made for research purposes, and generously granted permission to reproduce pages of Benjamin's MS; I would like to thank Frau Ursula Marx in particular for her help and advice.

Dr. Johannes Steizinger, Berlin, was very kind in offering me a copy of his dissertation on the youthful Walter Benjamin, and in expressing encouragement for my undertaking.

I would also like to acknowledge Hans Schüller of the Geschichts- und Altertumsverein Mayen (for information about C. Friedrich Heinle and other members of his family); Inge Münstermann of the Stadtarchiv Arnsberg (Westfalen; for confirming Wolf Heinle's date of birth); the helpful staff of the Zeitungsabteilung of the Staatsbibliothek Berlin; and Heidi

Buschhaus of the Deutsches Litaraturarchiv Marbach (for providing me with a photocopy of the Loewenson MS). I am most grateful to Petra Herzog, Aachen, who volunteered to visit local schools and libraries in search of more information about Fritz Heinle's school years there.

As with past Benjamin projects, I feel once again indebted to an old friend, Dr. Ronald G.G. Knox. Through him I am aware of how little I understand of religion, and how much more I ought to understand. Indeed, translating Benjamin's sonnets means entering into a world that seems to answer to a veiled personal observance, and the translator must be grateful for every clue which comes his way. I would also like to thank Ron for suggestions as to classical references in Sonnet 25.

Two young innocents agreed to read my introductory essay without necessarily knowing what they were getting into. I would like to thank Logan Strosahl and Nicolas Lobo, a.k.a. Nick D. Love, for their good will and industriousness, and for their many thoughtful comments. I am also indebted to Rebecca Wolff for having undertaken to review my work, and in particular the Essay which introduces this volume. Her interest led to much improvement of the whole.

My partner (and now spouse) Joseph Holtzman has always made sure to let me know how thoroughly he supports anything I do. This translation project was no exception, and I remain profoundly grateful.

Finally, I would like to dedicate this book to Matthew Stadler, the publisher of my previous Benjamin translations. I hope that, in some small way, what I have done here lives up to Matthew and his values.

ABOUT THE TRANSLATOR

Carl Skoggard has also produced translations and commentaries for Walter Benjamin's *Berliner Kindheit um 1900* (Berlin Childhood circa 1900) and *Berliner Chronik* (The 'Berlin Chronicle' Notices), and most recently, a first English version of Siegfried Kracauer's novel *Georg*. Previously he served as the staff writer for *Nest: A Quarterly of Interiors* and as an editor for the Répértoire International de la Littérature Musicale, with responsibility for German materials. His translation of *Ein Jahr in Arkadien*, an 1805 gay fiction by Duke August of Saxe-Gotha and Altenburg, appeared in 1999 as *Year in Arcadia*.

CHRISTIAN A. WOLLIN

AFTERWORD

THE TASK OF THE SONNETEER:
WALTER BENJAMIN'S POETRY AS A MANIFOLD TRADITION

I.

In her 1968 essay on Walter Benjamin, Hannah Arendt offers a concise definition of tradition: "Insofar as the past has been transmitted as tradition, it possesses authority; insofar as authority presents itself historically, it becomes tradition."[1] In this context, tradition may be described as the totality of discourses transmitted from any past to any present. Yet tradition only ever becomes tradition when and if the present actively engages with its discursive volume by means of archival preservation and collection, of philological editing, of commentary, or of critique. With tradition, then, the past's ability to have an impact on the present is at stake. Or, to put it differently: Tradition is a specific relation between present and past,

---

1   Hannah Arendt, "Introduction. Walter Benjamin: 1892–1940," transl. Harry Zohn, in Walter Benjamin, *Illuminations*, ed. Hannah Arendt (New York: Schocken Books, 2007), 38.

articulated as the present's decision on the extent to which the past is given authority over itself, a decision which every present must make anew for its own time. Accordingly, the practices and attitudes subsumed under tradition codify the specific ways in which the discourses traditioned (to use a now rare term) are retained by, and remain authoritative for, the present approaching them.

Benjamin's relationship with tradition shapes his intellectual profile fundamentally, and essential modes of his thinking and writing proceed from its conceptual configuration. His parting look at the domain of tradition is left to the "Angelus Novus." Among the "images and allegories" that, as Benjamin professed in *Berlin Childhood around 1900*, "preside over my thought,"[2] this "New Angel" famously occupies the place of the primus inter pares. He emerges from Paul Klee's 1920 painting of the same name, which Benjamin acquired in 1921,[3] and he makes his most

---

2   Benjamin's sonnets are quoted after Carl Skoggard's translations, with each quote indicating the number and verse(s) of the respective poem. Unless indicated otherwise, Benjamin's writings and letters are quoted after the following critical editions: Walter Benjamin, *Gesammelte Schriften*, eds. Rolf Tiedemann and Hermann Schweppenhäuser. 14 vols. Revised edition. (Frankfurt/M.: Suhrkamp Verlag 1991 — henceforth abbreviated as 'GS'); Walter Benjamin, *Werke und Nachlaß. Kritische Gesamtausgabe*, eds. Christoph Gödde and Henri Lonitz in cooperation with the Walter Benjamin Archiv. 21 vols. (Berlin: Suhrkamp Verlag 2008ff.—henceforth abbreviated as 'WuN'); Walter Benjamin, *Selected Writings*, eds. Howard Eiland and Michael W. Jennings. 4 vols. (Cambridge, MA, London, England: The Belknap Press of Harvard University Press, 2003–2006—henceforth abbreviated as 'SW'; unless indicated otherwise, all English translations are taken from this edition); Walter Benjamin, *Gesammelte Briefe*, eds. Christoph Gödde and Henri Lonitz. 6 vols. (Frankfurt/M.: Suhrkamp Verlag, 1995–2000—henceforth abbreviated as 'GB').—SW 3, 345.

3   For the complex passage of Klee's painting through Benjamin's life and thought, cf. Gershom Scholem, "Walter Benjamin and his Angel," in Gershom Scholem, *On Jews and Judaism in Crisis. Selected Essays*, ed. Werner A. Dannhauser (New York: Schocken Books 1987), 208–214.

prominent appearance in *On the Concept of History* (1939/40). In the ninth thesis of Benjamin's posthumous philosophical epitaph, the "Angelus Novus" undergoes his final metamorphosis. Conceived as the after-image of a twofold historical caesura, the German-Soviet Non-Aggression Pact of August 1939 and the subsequent outbreak of the Second World War, he now becomes the "Angel of History."[4] His solitary figure faces what Benjamin calls "catastrophe in permanence,"[5] the "catastrophe [that] is the continuum of history"[6]:

> "Where a chain of events appears before *us*, *he* sees one single catastrophe, which keeps piling wreckage upon wreckage and hurls it at his feet. The angel would like to stay, awaken the dead, and make whole what has been smashed. But a storm is blowing from Paradise and has got caught in his wings; it is so strong that the angel can no longer close them. This storm drives him irresistibly into the future to which his back is turned, while the pile of debris before him grows toward the sky. What we call progress is *this* storm."[7]

Benjamin's panorama of perpetual destruction and death is the transhistoric equivalent of what Hannah Arendt termed the "break in our tradition."[8] For Arendt, Benjamin had already become a seismographer of its

---

4   WuN 14, 35 (my translation).

5   SW 4, 164.

6   WuN 14, 133 (my translation).

7   SW 4, 392.

8   Hannah Arendt, "Tradition and the Modern Age," in Hannah Arendt: *Between Past and Future. Eight Exercises in Political Thought* (New York, London: Penguin Books 2006),

emergence in the 1920s. She located this "break" at the moment when, in Nazi Germany and Soviet Russia, "totalitarian movements, through ideology and terror, crystallized into a new form of government and domination."[9] Arendt furthermore held that Benjamin had reacted to this unfolding process by "discover[ing] new ways of dealing with the past,"[10] namely "that the transmissibility of the past had been replaced by its citability and that in place of its authority there had arisen a strange power to settle down, piecemeal, in the present [...]."[11] During the 1930s, Benjamin did indeed increasingly shift his reflective focus to the notion of tradition. With "aura," he conceptualized a dimension that described his present in terms of its ever-diminishing ability to access tradition and to tradition its own experiences, charting the trajectory of (artistic) modernity as the progressive loss of "aura."[12]

The last decade of his life, however, saw Benjamin also working on three projects that present a more complex face to Arendt's clear-cut diagnosis that he was supplanting the lost authority of tradition by quoting the

---

26.—In 1944, Arendt became the first person to quote this passage from the ninth thesis of *On the Concept of History*, from an early manuscript version Benjamin had entrusted to her in Paris, and which in 1941 she brought with her to New York; cf. Hannah Arendt, "Franz Kafka. A Revaluation on the Occasion of the Twentieth Anniversary of His Death, 1944," *Partisan Review* 11 (1944): 412–422, 417.

9   Arendt, "Tradition and the Modern Age," 26.

10   Arendt, "Introduction," 38.

11   Ibid.

12   Cf. *Experience and Poverty* (193—SW 2.2, 731–736), the various versions of *The Work of Art in the Age of Its Technological Reproducibility* (1935–39—SW 3, 101-133, gives its second version), *The Storyteller: Observations on the Works of Nikolai Leskov* (1936—SW 3, 143–166), and *On Some Motifs in Baudelaire* (1939—SW 4, 313–355).

past. To be sure, the notion of "citability" and the practice of quotation are at the core of the *Arcades Project* and *On the Concept of History*. Yet the *Arcades Project* may equally be described as Benjamin's boldly confident attempt to tradition the entire 19th century within the confines of a single textual montage of quotations. In the same way, *On the Concept of History* marks the culminating point of his effort to furnish the proletariat with a philosophy of history and a historiographic practice that can truly articulate the "tradition of the oppressed"[13]. And finally, there is *German Men and Women*, the selection and commentary of 25 letters written between 1783 and 1883 which Benjamin published under the pseudonym of "Detlef Holz" in 1936. All three projects highlight the tension that defines the final phase of his life and work, which ended abruptly with his suicide in September 1940 while fleeing the Nazi German occupation of France. In many ways, the years leading up to his death are Benjamin's intellectual *akmé*, coinciding with his sovereign command over the discursive stores of tradition. Yet the philosophical intensity with which he was invested into tradition is inseparable from the political "constellation of dangers"[14] he was exposed to, threatening his own life and work no less than tradition as such. He witnessed the triumphant European rise of what he summarily called "fascism"[15] in Italy, Germany, Austria, Portugal, and Spain. And he distanced himself more and more from Stalin's Soviet Russia, the sworn ideological enemy of Nazi Germany that would turn into its obliging ally in 1939. From this perspective, the *Arcades Project* and *On the Concept of History* are perhaps also fashioned as vessels of

---

13   SW 5, 392.

14   WuN 14, 127.

15   SW 5, 392.

tradition in the sense of *German Men and Women*, which Benjamin called an "ark that I built when the fascist Flood began to rise."[16] Conceptually, his will of traditioning the past and of preserving tradition articulates itself most forcefully in the notion of "remembrance"[17] ("Eingedenken"[18]). In the *Arcades Project* and *On the Concept of History*, its term designates an attitude towards history that radically departs from the disinterested "sine ira et studio"[19] of conventional historiography. Against the latter, Benjamin holds emphatically that "history is not simply a science but also and not least a form of remembrance *<Eingedenken>*. What science has 'determined,' remembrance can modify. Such mindfulness can make the incomplete (happiness) into something complete, and the complete (suffering) into something incomplete."[20] As a first "messianic"[21] step in redeeming humanity from history's "catastrophe in permanence," Benjamin tasks the historian with "incompleting" its past eventscapes of loss, suffering, injustice, and disappointed hopes. The historian can fulfill this task by traditioning and actualizing them as completely as possible, and thereby becomes the inverted double of the "Angel of History."

---

16   WuN 10, 174 and 175 (my translation).

17   Walter Benjamin, *The Arcades Project*, transl. Howard Eiland and Kevin McLaughlin (Cambridge, MA, London, England: The Belknap Press of Harvard University Press, 2002), 471(N8, 1).

18   GS 5.1, 589 (N8, 1)—Although Benjamin declares "remembrance" to be anchored in Jewish tradition (cf. WuN 14, 142), he in fact elaborates a notion by Ernst Bloch, his friend and fellow Jewish-German philosopher; cf. Ernst Bloch, *Thomas Münzer als Theologe der Revolution* (Frankfurt/M.: Suhrkamp Verlag 1967), 14f.

19   Cornelius Tacitus, *The Annals. The Reigns of Tiberius, Claudius, and Nero*, trans. J. C. Yardley (Oxford, New York: Oxford University Press 1972), 49 (I, 1).

20   Walter Benjamin, *The Arcades Project*, 471(N8, 1).

21   SW 4, 390.

Within the conceptual force-field of "remembrance," Benjamin's seventy-two sonnets, probably composed between 1914/15 and 1925,[22] must inevitably appear to have always been guarded by the "Angel of History." The agency of "remembrance" makes itself already felt in Carl Skoggard's captivating tableau of the complex biographical constellations from which Benjamin's "sonnets of mourning"[23] emerge.[24] It tells of the intellectual and emotional intensity of his involvement with the German "youth movement" up to 1914, of his close friendship and conflicts with the poet Fritz Heinle against the ideological backdrop of this movement, and finally of the catastrophic dénouement of this formative period of Benjamin's life in the event of Heinle's suicide on August 8, 1914, shortly after the outbreak of the First World War. This sequence frames Heinle suggestively as the default protagonist of Benjamin's first paradigmatic narrative of "remembrance," as told by his cycle of sonnets. By contrast, my reading of Benjamin's poems will attempt to move their textual trajectory away from the ever-present gravitational pull of his philosophical conceptions of historiography and history. I will focus on Benjamin the sonneteer, and I will constellate his poems inside the conceptual sphere of tradition, of which "remembrance" constitutes a special form.

---

22 Cf. GS 7.2, 573f.

23 Cf. Carl Skoggard, "Introduction," p. 13 in this volume.

24 Cf. Skoggard, "Introduction," pp.15–22 and 31f. in this volume.

II.

Benjamin's sonnets do not begin with themselves, but with a motto. They are preceded by an entire stanza from Hölderlin's seminal late poem *Patmos* (1802–03), which sets their hermeneutical stage. Composed as a paratactical question, this stanza ends with condensing and reduplicating itself into a simple formula: "what is this?"[25]. It asks for the essence, the "whatness" of a thing or a situation, seeking closure in terms of a definition. At the center of its inquiry is a threefold sequence of events which sharply oscillates between presence and absence, between past and present: First, the death of a male "person"[26] or "demigod"[27] who embodied a maximum of "beauty"[28] no less than a "miracle"[29] (or "wonder"). Subsequently, the coexistence of the "demigod" and "his friends"[30] has given way to an impossible "memory"[31] of their communal experience. Finally, death has "blown away"[32] all traces of the wondrous manifestation of utmost beauty from the world, and with it all "immortal"[33] presences in it. In *Patmos* and elsewhere, Hölderlin thus tries to decipher the meaning behind the sud-

---

25 Friedrich Hölderlin, *Poems and Fragments*, trans. Michael Hamburger. Fourth bilingual edition (London: Anvil Press Poetry 2004), 559.

26 Ibid.

27 Ibid.

28 Ibid.

29 Ibid.

30 Ibid.

31 Hölderlin, *Poems and Fragments*, 558 (my translation).

32 Hölderlin, *Poems and Fragments*, 559.

33 Ibid.

den disappearance of a qualitative maximum, ontological or metaphysical, from the world, and gauges the intramundane impact of this event. For the sonnets, Benjamin programmatically appropriates Hölderlin's hermeneutics of loss. But where *Patmos* explicitly addresses the passion of Christ, Benjamin's quotation suppresses this reference so as to allow for a displacement of the poem's (semi-)divine focal point to another figure. His opening poem firmly enshrines its name, both materially and metaphysically, in the cycle's textual space (Sonnet 1, l. 13f.): "Plant in me thy sacred Name instead | Name without image Amen without end." Perhaps these verses already allude to Benjamin's theory of Adamitic language, developed around 1916, in which names hold the essence of the thing or being which is named.[34] Their (un-)named holy name is that of Fritz Heinle. His life and death are at the discursive center of Benjamin's sonnets and their realm of "lofty reflective mourning."[35] In its bounds, Heinle's character performs various Hölderlinian parts of syncretistic antique and Christian reference, all of which transform him into a presence of the highest ontological magnitude. He is "the Beautiful one" (Sonnet 45, l. 1), or simply the "most beautiful of men" (Sonnet 12, l. 14), and "the gods shall keep him in their hands | For whom they send alive is ridiculed and mocked." (Sonnet 20, l. 13f.) Moreover, the sonnets address Heinle in a manner similar to the Lord's Prayer (Sonnet 16), or indeed as the "redeemer" (Sonnet 29, l. 14—"Heiland"), "who is risen" (Sonnet 31, l. 14).

---

34 Cf. *On Language as Such and on the Language of Man* (ca. 1916), SW 1, 62–74.

35 Clemens Brentano's formula for the essence of Hölderlin's late poetry, coined in a letter to Philipp Otto Runge, Berlin, 21 January 1810: "Niemals ist vielleicht hohe betrachtende Trauer so herrlich ausgesprochen worden." (Philipp Otto Runge, *Die Begier nach der Möglichkeit neuer Bilder. Briefwechsel und Schriften zur bildenden Kunst*, ed. Hannelore Gärtner [Leipzig: Verlag Reclam jun. 1982], 309—my translation.)

With his sonnets, Benjamin thus appears to answer Hölderlin's query from *Patmos* by rewriting Heinle's life and suicide as something of a poetical myth that bears testimony, canonizes, and traditions at the same time. And indeed, the sonnets constitute the largest extant part of Benjamin's project to establish Fritz Heinle's place inside tradition and to secure the discursive preservation of the man and his work for future times. But a peculiar *desoeuvrement* seems to haunt the material, editorial, and critical components of Benjamin's undertaking from the very beginning.[36] After Heinle's suicide in 1914, Benjamin assembled a complete archive of his surviving writings. It was left behind in Berlin when he emigrated from Nazi Germany to Paris in September 1933 and has been lost ever since.[37] In the early 1920s, Benjamin had intended to publish Heinle's writings both as a separate volume and in selections in his journal *Angelus Novus*.[38] However, the plans for his book, just as the journal itself, never materialized. Moreover, the publication of Heinle's work was to include a "preface"[39] or "introduction."[40] Yet Benjamin never wrote or finished this text, which

---

36   In his preface to the first German edition of those writings and letters by Heinle that were preserved by his friends and by Benjamin, Giorgio Agamben states: "In everything that concerns Heinle there is an unconscious inclination for loss." (Christoph Friedrich Heinle, *Lyrik und Prosa*, ed. Johannes Steizinger [Berlin: Kulturverlag Kadmos, 2016], 19, n.37 [my translation].)

37   Cf. Benjamin's letter to Gretel Adorno, GB 6, 175 (Paris, November 1, 1938).

38   Cf. Benjamin's letters to Gershom Scholem, GB 2, 197 (Berlin, October 4, 1921) and GB 2, 207 (Berlin, November 8, 1921); to Richard Weißbach, GB 2, 218 (Berlin, December 3, 1921), GB 2, 244 (Berlin, April 16, 1922), and GB 2, 262 (Berlin, June 30, 1922).

39   GB 2, 249 (letter to Richard Weißbach, Berlin, April 18, 1922—my translation).

40   GB 2, 289 (letter to Florens Christian Rang, Heidelberg, December 3, 1922—my translation).

would also have constituted his only sustained critical treatment of poetry as genre, and its materials have been lost as well.[41] What remains of Heinle's person and writings in Benjamin's own author-text is an isolated critical dictum in the *Berlin Chronicle* ("Fritz Heinle was a Poet"[42]), scattered poetic fragments and testimonia (much in the ennobled sense of their pre-Socratic counterparts), esoteric allusions, marked as such by himself or retrospectively by Gershom Scholem, in certain texts[43]—and the sonnets.

Benjamin's poems entertain a relationship with tradition that sets them very much apart from the kind of formal and reflective sophistication to be found in the *Arcades Project* or *On the Concept of History*. Referring to his evolution as a writer and thinker, Theodor W. Adorno asserted that Benjamin "was not the talent that formed in silence, but the genius who, desperately swimming against the current, came into his own."[44] At least in literary terms, the opposite can be said of Benjamin the sonneteer. He clearly preferred to swim with the current, immersing himself in the depths of what he then recognized as authoritative poetical tradition. In the 1910s, Benjamin's frame of reference was controlled by the poet Stefan George, one of the defining figures of early German modernism.[45] In 1928, Benja-

---

41   The last traces of this projected text can be found in two letters of Benjamin (to Scholem, GB 2, 299 [Braunfels, December 30, 1922], and to Florens Christian Rang, GB 2, 355 [Berlin, October 7, 1923]), and in *Berlin Chronicle* (1932–SW 2.2, 604/GS 6, 477).

42   SW 2.2, 604 (translation modified).

43   The most important among these esoteric references are *Two Poems by Friedrich Hölderlin* (1914/15—SW 1, 18-36) and Dostoevsky's *The Idiot* (SW 1, 78-81).

44   Theodor W. Adorno, "A l'écart de tous les courants," in Theodor W. Adorno, *Über Walter Benjamin. Aufsätze, Artikel, Briefe*, ed. Rolf Tiedemann (Frankfurt/M.: Suhrkamp Verlag 1990), 103.

45   A selection of Stefan George's poetry is available in translation: Stefan George, *Poems*, transl. Ernst Morwitz, C. N. Valhope (Schocken Books: New York 1967).

min responded to a round call for "autobiographical notes" on "George's position in German intellectual life"[46] occasioned by the poet's sixtieth birthday. In this first of two critical retrospects devoted to him,[47] Benjamin declared: "Thus, George's impact on my life is bound to poetry in its most vital sense. How I came under his dominion and how it disintegrated within me, it did all happen inside the space of poetry and in the friendship of a poet."[48] The "poet" in question is Fritz Heinle, while "poetry" encompasses both George's oeuvre and poetry as such. Their triple constellation shapes Benjamin's own poetry to its core. In his retrospect, he may have chosen to let his emancipation from George coincide with Heinle's death in August 1914, stating that in subsequent months "the poems he had left behind came to occupy the few spaces inside me where poems could still have a decisive impact."[49] But the discursive factuality of Benjamin's sonnets points to a different state of affairs. They do not articulate a break with George. Nor do they conform to any of the six "revisionary ratios"[50] Harold Bloom introduced to describe the intertextual ways in which poets stage literary rivalries and conflicts in their writing.[51] The sonnets are no "Umdichtungen" ("reworkings") of George in the agonistic sense of the term by which the latter referred to his own translations from the West-

---

46 GS 2.3, 1431 (my translation).

47 Benjamin's second text on the poet is *Stefan George in Retrospect. On a New Study of the Poet* (1932 — cf. SW 2.2, 706–711).

48 GS 2.2, 623 (my translation).

49 Ibid.

50 Harold Bloom, *The Anxiety of Influence: A Theory of Poetry* (Oxford, New York: Oxford University Press 1997), 8.

51 Cf. Harold Bloom, *The Anxiety of Influence*.

ern canon. Rather, they suggest an echo chamber filled with voices almost all of which have passed through George's poetical amplifier. Benjamin's sonnets dramatize the hold George continued to have over him through a structure reminiscent of Louis Althusser's "mirror-stage" of ideology. Benjamin as poet, they suggest, can only insert himself into tradition, can only confer authority on his own writing by (mis-)recognizing himself in the absolute literary instance of George.[52]

If the authorial relation between Benjamin and George is thus defined by the simultaneity of distance and proximity, this tension translates itself into his sonnets as a powerful structural sense of dislocation. Benjamin's poems never flatly or, for that matter, consummately imitate. Instead, they lead the reader into textual landscapes whose sceneries, situations and personae, along with their gestures, more often than not seem to have been transplanted from elsewhere. This "coming from elsewhere" is, of course, essential to literature under the conceptual banner of intertextuality. Yet with Benjamin's sonnets, there is only a limited number of occasions where he successfully neutralizes the agency of dislocation. Altogether, their poetical domain is the latent distance they have always-already taken up to themselves; it lies within the spatial vector of their displacement. Benjamin's resolve to insert himself into poetical tradition, informed perhaps by his metaphysics of poetic language as naming,[53] is at odds with the scope of his ability to match this gesture artistically. A letter to his friend

---

52   Cf. Louis Althusser: "Ideology and Ideological State Apparatuses. (Notes Towards an Investigation)," in Louis Althusser, *Lenin and Philosophy and other essays*, trans. Ben Brewster (New York: Monthly Review Press 2001), 85–132.

53   Cf. *On Language as Such and on the Language of Man* (1916), SW 1, 73: "[T]he language of poetry is partly, if not solely, founded on the name language of man [...]."

and fellow poet Ernst Schoen, written in June 1916, captures this tension between Benjamin's attitude of conceptual authority and the fact of his poetic apprenticeship:

> "I believe I am allowed to talk about your poems
> because they are so kindred to me in their striving to
> not embrace the pure body of language, but to behold
> it from afar, through unadulterated air. Without unduly
> extolling your work and mine, I believe I can say how
> infinitely essential the sheer measure of labor contained
> in it is for our growth. [...] Purity is the ultimate goal
> that *our* work can set itself as of yet."[54]

Benjamin's will to "purity" and his poetics of linguistic distance are compromised and fulfilled in equal measure by the sonnets' structural purity of dislocation. Above all, it is the pervasive latency of its force that gives his poems their individuality and confers a strange beauty upon them. At the same time, Benjamin's involuntary poetics of citational latency does not indicate a shift in his relationship with tradition of the kind Arendt diagnosed for the 1930s. Through the death of Heinle, he may mourn the dissolution of the German "youth movement" during the First World War, and the disappearance of the corresponding discursive world of "youth." But his default mode of textual dislocation does not react to a crisis of tradition in the way T. S. Eliot's *The Waste Land* (1922) did in the aftermath of the war. Benjamin's sonnets are not "[t]hese fragments I have shored against

---

54   GB I, 329 (To Ernst Schoen, Seeshaupt, July 20, 1916—my translation).

my ruins."[55] Rather, their covert bricolage of "auratic" literary spoils places them in the unlikely vicinity of the first versions of Ezra Pound's *Cantos*, published in 1917.[56] The incompatible aesthetics of Benjamin and Pound converge in affirming the enduring authority of tradition against the event of the war. And in each of them, this affirmation takes a poetical form resonant with the theatrical manner in which, to return the metaphor to its origin, the Middle Ages and the Renaissance reused artifacts (*spolia*) from Greco-Roman antiquity for their own architecture and art.

In Benjamin's case, these spoils can mostly be traced back to the instance of Stefan George, both as originator and mediator. To begin with, there is his choice of the Petrarchan sonnet, one of Western poetry's most canonized forms. At first, it may seem likely Benjamin was aware that, at roughly the same time of his own writing, three prominent German and Austrian poets had also turned their attention to the sonnet. Between 1907 and 1923, Rainer Maria Rilke, Georg Heym, and Georg Trakl used it as a somehow voided form that nevertheless offered enough structural resilience to accommodate the centrifugal forces of their high modernist vision.[57] With Benjamin, who at the time probably had limited knowledge of Rilke's texts and was seemingly ignorant of Heym and Trakl, this implicit conflict is however reversed. In choosing the sonnet form, he signals his

---

55   T. S. Eliot, "The Waste Land," in T. S. Eliot, *The Complete Plays and Poems* (London: Faber and Faber 1969), 75, v. 430.

56   Cf. Ezra Pound, *Early Writings. Poems and Prose*, ed. Ira B. Nadel (London, New York: Penguin Books 2005), 145–162.

57   For Rilke, cf. his cycles *Neue Gedichte* (1907/08) and *Die Sonette an Orpheus* (1923); for Heym, cf. his first volume of poetry, *Der ewige Tag* (1911); for Trakl, cf. such poems as "Afra," "Dämmerung," "Dezembersonett," "Ein Herbstabend," "Märchen," "Traum des Bösen," and "Verfall."

untimely allegiance to a poetical modernity curated by George and situates himself at a certain distance from the literary avant-gardes of his present. While George wrote relatively few sonnets, two of his most authoritative "Umdichtungen" ("reworkings") are centered around the Petrarchan and Shakespearean modes of the sonnet: *Baudelaire. Flowers of Evil* (1901), and *Shakespeare Sonnets* (1909). Another integral element of this configuration is Benjamin's own translation of Baudelaire's *Tableaux parisiens*, the second part of *Les Fleurs du mal*. Published as a book in 1923, he very probably began working on it simultaneously to the sonnets.[58] And lastly, it may also have been through George's selective translations that he became acquainted with Stéphane Mallarmé, another master sonneteer who reverberates in the echo chamber of Benjamin's poetry.

Once Hölderlin is added to this constellation of texts and authors, it becomes apparent that Benjamin created the sonnets' space of dislocation from the coordinates of a poetical canon championed by George. Though he may have gone beyond the instance of George by subsequently including Rimbaud, Rilke, and Heym, they would ultimately remain at the margin. And although Hölderlin emblazons Benjamin's cycle paratextually with the stanza-motto taken from *Patmos* and its topoi of loss and tradition, he cannot be said to inform them poetically. Hölderlin's powerful fusion of the sublime and the simple, which defines *Patmos* and his late poetry of the 1800s in general, is notably absent from the sonnets. Equally absent is his masterly command of rhythm, whose deceptively conversational flow musicalizes even his most complex syntactical con-

---

58   In January 1924, Benjamin wrote to Hugo von Hofmannsthal that "nine years have passed" between his first attempts at translating Baudelaire and the publication of the finished translation in 1923; cf. GB II, 410 (Berlin, January 10, 1924).

structions. Whenever Benjamin chooses to obscure or condense linguistic structures, both syntactically and by eliminating all punctuation, he rather invokes the authoritative precedent of Mallarmé, whom George emulated in turn.[59] With the possible exception of Sonnet 61, the dislocation of Benjamin's poetic simulacra, however, tends to widen the artistic gap between their models and themselves. Where Mallarmé and George achieve semantic levitation through syntactical and grammatical harshness, Benjamin often seems to only simulate such effects and to mask with the absence of punctuation moments of prosodic monotony instead. A single element from the sonnets' lexicon may serve as a last paradigm of how Benjamin generates their metonymical web of textual dislocation. Sonnet 3 speaks of "his cheek | Which swims the azure as a glowing cloud" (l. 7/8). The German original employs the rare term "im Azur" (Sonnet 3, l. 8), a color noun derived from the French, and usually associated with poetic use. Yet again, Benjamin's lexical choice leads back to George's "Umdichtungen" of Baudelaire's *Les Fleurs du mal* and of Mallarmé and to various central poems by the two French poets. Thus, in *L'Albatros*, Baudelaire addresses the sea-bird in the plural, as "ces rois de l'azur,"[60] with George translating the formula as "die herrn im azur."[61] And in Baudelaire's *La Beauté*, the personification of beauty declares: "Je trône dans l'azur comme un

---

59   Cf. Mallarmé's famous group of sonnets, *Plusieurs sonnets* (1887). For George's relationship to Mallarmé, cf. Stefan George/Stéphane Mallarmé, *Briefwechsel und Übertragungen*, ed. Enrico De Angelis (Göttingen: Wallstein Verlag 2013).

60   Charles Baudelaire, "L'Albatros," in Charles Baudelaire, *Les Fleurs du Mal*, ed. John E. Jackson (Paris: Le Livre de Poche 1972), 54 (l. 6).

61   Stefan George, Baudelaire. *Die Blumen des Bösen. Umdichtungen* (Stuttgart: Klett-Cotta 1983), 12, l. 6.

sphinx incompris,"[62] while *La Chevelure* likens female hair to "l'azur du ciel immense et rond,"[63] which George renders with "azur-himmel rund und schrankenleer."[64] But "l'azur" features no less conspicuously in Mallarmé's poetry. It traverses his eclogue *L'Aprés-midi d'un faune* (1876) as well as the *Scène de Hérodiade* (1896) and also George's translation *Herodias* (1904). His version of Mallarmé's *Apparition* transposes "l'azur des corolles"[65] as "azurne kelche."[66] And last but not least, there is *L'Azur* (1864), which closes with the apostrophe: "*Je suis hanté. L'Azur! l'Azur! l'Azur! l'Azur!*"[67]

III.

In his 1928 retrospect on George, Benjamin develops a complex configuration of poetry, lived experience, and memory. He begins with the axiomatic statement that it is "the privilege and the unspeakable happiness of youth [...] to legitimize itself through verses, to be able to invoke verses in dispute and in love [...]."[68] And he goes on to name George as the poet whom he and his circle of friends in the youth movement had chosen to fulfill

---

62   Charles Baudelaire, "La Beauté," in Charles Baudelaire, *Les Fleurs du Mal*, 67 (l. 5).

63   Charles Baudelaire, "La Chevelure," in Charles Baudelaire, *Les Fleurs du Mal*, 73 (l. 27).

64   Stefan George, Baudelaire. *Die Blumen des Bösen. Umdichtungen*, 39, l. 27.

65   Stéphane Mallarmé, *Poésies*, ed. Bertrand Marchal (Paris: Gallimard 1992), 7, l. 4.

66   Stéphane Mallarmé, "Erscheinung," trans. Stefan George, in Stefan George, *Zeitgenössische Dichter. Übertragungen. Zweiter Teil* (Stuttgart: Klett-Cotta 2001), 32 (l. 4).

67   Stéphane Mallarmé, *Poésies*, 21, l. 36.

68   GS 2.2, 623 (my translation).

this existential function. Benjamin moreover speaks of the "bond"—he uses the word "verbunden"[69]—that George's poetry established between his friends and himself. But he emphasizes that this 'bond' did not reside in the poet and his poems, but rather in a "power"[70] manifesting itself as much through George and his work as they, in turn, were indispensable for its manifestation. The factuality of death—"none of them is alive today," Benjamin wrongly states[71]—transforms the symbiosis between his poetry, the "power," and the lived experience of himself and his friends into something else which is at once similar and dissimilar. Benjamin's second *Retrospect on George*, written in 1932, captures the originary configuration of multiple presences in the formula "a youth which lived in those poems."[72] Having passed through death, the subsequent structure rests on the temporalizing agency of memory and its intricate play between absence and presence. Now "youth," Benjamin's shorthand for the emotional and intellectual sphere collectively inhabited by his friends and himself until 1914, no longer "lives in those poems." Instead, the draft notes for the 1928 text describe how these habitats have become radically singularized, taking on a new intensity of concretion in the process: "How the image of a human being attached itself [*sich...verbunden hat*] to each of these poems."[73] In this way, Benjamin pairs specific poems by George with his wife Dora

---

69   GS 2.2, 622 (my translation).

70   GS 2.2, 623 (my translation).

71   GS 2.2, 622f. (my translation).—When Benjamin wrote and published his retrospect in 1928, the persons he alluded to were still alive, with the exception of Rika Seligson and Fritz Heinle.

72   SW 2.2, 710 (translation modified).

73   GS 2.3, 1430 (my translation).

Benjamin, Fritz Heinle, Rika Seligson, Simon Guttmann (a protagonist of the Berlin youth movement), and finally with himself. The published final version replaces Dora Benjamin with Heinle's lover, Rika Seligson, who is linked to George's translations from Dante's *Divine Comedy*, and suppresses all personal names along with Benjamin's reference to himself.

The reflexive space of Benjamin's retrospect, then, reconfigures George's poems into powerful mnemonic devices designed to withstand the caesura of death. Each poetic text he cites becomes a memorial holding the "image" of the individual who once recited it. For Fritz Heinle, Benjamin describes this process as follows: "Just as 'Gemahnt dich noch das schöne bildnis dessen' ['Does the beautiful portrait of him still remind you'] does indeed call on me to remind myself because my friend, by loving it, gave it some of his features."[74] His descriptions imply that the "image" unfailingly captures the essential features of a human being, or, in the cases of Rika Seligson and Dora Benjamin, the essence of a relationship or the biographical kairos of love. With "image," Benjamin thus transposes the semantic intensity of the ancient Greek term *eikón*, whose meanings comprise "*likeness*, image, whether picture or statue," "*image in a mirror*," and "*living image, representation*."[75] Yet in his case, it always does so in an emphatically subjective fashion, preserving the "truth" of the individual in question as crystallized through Benjamin's own emotional and intellectual investment into her or him. The retrospect's internal temporality of memory introduces an element of ambiguity to this structure. It cannot be decided

---

74   GS 2.2, 624 (my translation).—For the poem itself, cf. Stefan George, *Das Jahr der Seele* (Stuttgart: Klett-Cotta 1982), 40.

75   Henry George Liddell, Robert Scott, *A Greek-English Lexicon*, rev. Henry Stuart Jones (Oxford: Clarendon Press 1940), 485.

whether the individuals' essences revealed themselves to Benjamin at the very moment the poems were recited, or whether he discovered them at some later time, as a result of memory's work itself. At any rate, Benjamin thereby creates a multidimensional "scenography"[76] of memory which preserves and traditions human beings as the present totality of image, voice, rhythm, gestures, attitude, words, situational specificity, space, and time. By subsuming this complex arrangement under the term "image," Benjamin may appear to privilege the atemporal, stationary dimension of the visual in a Platonic fashion. But its persistence and immediacy as memory results primarily from the agency of poetic prosody, which, as Hans Ulrich Gumbrecht has argued, is able to give a form to the temporal object of a poem.[77] Possibly alluding to Benjamin's distinction between "homogeneous, empty time"[78] and the time of "remembrance," Gumbrecht contrasts two temporal modes with each other. On the one hand, there is the "normal" and formless time of "chronos."[79] But there is also "kairos,"[80] time formed as rhythm, and articulated through poetry, music, etc. Because such "kairotic" rhythms can be repeated in a virtually infinite manner, their elements are essentially simultaneous with each other, thus making available in the present any memories attached to these rhythms in the past. In Benjamin's case, the "kairotic" mode of time confers a form to

---

76   Roland Barthes, "Plaisir/écriture/lecture," in Roland Barthes, *Le grain de la voix. Entretiens* 1962-1980 (Paris: Éditions du Seuil 1981), 159 (my translation).

77   Cf. Hans Ulrich Gumbrecht, "Wozu sind Verse, Strophen und Reime gut?," *Digital/Pausen*, April 22, 2017 http://blogs.faz.net/digital/2017/04/22/wozu-sind-verse-strophen-und-reime-gut-1208/

78   SW 4, 396.

79   Hans Ulrich Gumbrecht, "Wozu sind Verse, Strophen und Reime gut?"

80   Ibid.

every individual he names because each of them has actualized the poem by reciting it. Only the temporalized performative space of recitation fuses individual bodies and patterns of rhythm, voices and spoken verses. It thereby medializes the presence of a human being in such a way that it can be preserved and traditioned as memory, through the poem's mnemonic *symbolon*. And Benjamin's "image" complex of poem and person does indeed bear a strong resemblance to the practice referred to by this antique Greek term. In the context of ancient Greek and Roman hospitality, individuals or families would codify their friendship by breaking up a ring, a coin, or a pottered tablet into two halves. These halves would then be divided among the friends, to be presented and joined together at every following meeting, also across generations.[81] In the same way, Benjamin's "image" becomes the hinge of emotional and intellectual investment, of presence and memory only after its two halves, poem and individual, have been brought together. George's poems can only function as mnemonic vehicles for Benjamin because they have incorporated the individuals who once recited them, and continue to do so in his present. Inversely, these individuals have been traditioned by them only because they at one point were drawn and then connected to the poems, the act of recitation being both cause and medium of this connection.

Benjamin's sonnets, it may seem at first, could not be farther removed from such intricate configurations of memory. As described above, their majority is shaped by the mode of poetic dislocation. But there is a second textual force that imposes itself on them as another agent of dislocation. Drawing on a finite number of poetical gestures and scenarios, each son-

---

81 Cf. Georg Picht, *Platons Dialoge "Nomoi" und "Symposion"* (Stuttgart: Klett-Cotta 1990), 543f.

net stages a variation of Benjamin's allegorical theatre of mourning for Heinle. Although it was Baudelaire's poetry that Benjamin characterized as "the baroque of banality,"[82] his formula strikes no less at the heart of his own work. Its repertoire of abstract significations allegorizes the process of dying and the event of death, which are contrasted with a corresponding set of allegorical representations of birth, life, and youth. Benjamin articulates this binarized semantic space with the help of heavily conventionalized allegorical elements, images and situations: the day's course from morning to night, the change of the seasons, a ship voyage (Sonnet 53), a chariot race (Sonnet 25), memory personified (Sonnet 9), the book of life (Sonnet 33), etc. In most poems, the ever-present agency of allegorical encoding thus applies itself to a topic of materials that, as it were, have always-already been allegorized. These dynamics limit the sonnets' capacity of "worldmaking"[83] (to use Nelson Goodman's term) because they suspend, or even eliminate, referential immediacy in terms of space, time and situational specificity. From this overall picture, four texts in Benjamin's cycle stand out. Sonnets 11, 36, 37, and 38 all share the setting of a town, established at the beginning of their opening stanza: "the white town" (Sonnet 11, l. 1), "beloved town" (Sonnet 36, l. 2), "the town" (Sonnet 37, l. 1) and "marchland town" (Sonnet 38, l. 1). For the diptych of nos. 36 and 37, the "town" may be identified as Freiburg, if "minster bells" (Sonnet 36, l. 7) and "minster" (Sonnet 37, l. 14) are contextualized with Benjamin's author-text: He first met Heinle in Freiburg, a Southern

---

82   GB 2, 411 (Letter to Hugo von Hofmannsthal, Berlin, January 10, 1924—my translation).

83   Cf. Nelson Goodman, *Ways of Worldmaking* (Indianapolis: Hackett Publishing Company 1978).

German town famous for its gothic cathedral, in 1913. The toponymical references "marchland town" ("Märkische Stadt," l. 1) and "Havelsee" (l. 5—an unspecified lake fed by the river Havel) situate Sonnet 38 in what was historically called the Mark Brandenburg, a key province of Prussia with Berlin at its center. No such concrete attribution, however, seems possible for "the white town" of Sonnet 11.

Benjamin's poetic townscapes resemble neither George's allegorical sites of cultural decay, nor do they emulate the total mobilization of metropolitan modernity by Baudelaire, Rilke, and Heym.[84] Each of the four sonnets constructs its abstract or individualized urban reference ("white town," Freiburg, "Märkische Stadt") as a "chronotope"[85] of memory intended for Fritz Heinle. Mikhail Bakhtin's concept of "chronotope" locates the intratextual configuration of space and time at the narrative heart of prose and drama.[86] While the Russian theorist himself did not apply his notion to poetry, its structural dynamic is nevertheless constitutive for Benjamin's group of urban sonnets. They articulate, as Bakhtin put it, "time as the fourth dimension of space."[87] Or, to rephrase him: These four poems spatialize time and they temporalize space, and they moreover anticipate the

---

84 For George, cf. "Die tote Stadt" and "Das Zeitgedicht" (2), both from *Der Siebente Ring* (1907); for Baudelaire, cf. such poems from *Les Fleurs du mal* as "Le soleil," "À une Passante," "Les Sept Vieillards" and "Le Crépuscule du soir"; for Rilke, cf. "Die Städte aber wollen nur das Ihre" (1903); and for Heym cf. "Berlin I–III" (1910), "Der Gott der Stadt" (1910), "Die Dämonen der Städte" (1910), and "Sehnsucht nach Paris" (1911).

85 Cf. Mikhail M. Bakhtin, "Forms of Time and of the Chronotope in the Novel," in Mikhail M. Bakhtin, *The Dialogic Imagination. Four Essays*, ed. Michael Holquist (Austin: University of Texas Press 1981), 84.

86 Cf. Bakhtin, "Forms of Time and of the Chronotope in the Novel," 84–258.

87 Bakhtin, "Forms of Time and of the Chronotope in the Novel," 84.

mnemonic "image" scenography of the 1928 autobiographical retrospect. The semantics of space is introduced through the sonnets' dominant frame of reference as they map the referential demarcation of "town" onto the textual boundaries of a poem. The semantics of time traverses each sonnet in different ways. Sonnet 11 gives a sequence of impressions charged with a sense of moving through urban space and of visiting different places in it. A similar scenario can be found in Sonnet 38, set mostly, however, in the surroundings of the "marchland town." Sonnet 36 loosely records the course and sights of a day at Freiburg. Sonnet 37 speaks of the act of returning to Freiburg, metaphorizing it through the double image of aural "echoes" (l. 3) and visual reflections in the minster's windows ("In panes of many tint such light did break," l. 11).

Taken by itself, this enumeration of elements may suggest that the four sonnets present time and space only in a default state of contiguity. Yet Benjamin fashions a set of spatiotemporal forms in which the synthesis of space and time materializes poetically as musical or musicalized rhythm. Thus, in Sonnet 11, "[a]s though with song was once the white town | with his footsteps filled" (l. 1–2), and under "the sullen sky | Which scorching overhung the ancient park | Where in the wave-ring ["Wellenschlag," literally: "wave beats," CAW] made by granted wishes | Sleep did round him flow a green flood [. . .]" (l. 4–7). The Freiburg depicted in Sonnet 36 is a place in which "laughed | The strikings [. . .] | Of those hours storing up the minster bells" (l. 5–7)[88]. But it does equally know times when "[n]ow trees fell silent and the wine in goblets sang | Inside our talk the rushing river whispers still" (l. 9–10). In Sonnet 38, the relative toponymical imme-

---

88 In *Freiburg minster*, a piece from *One-Way Street* (1928), Benjamin in a similar fashion identifies Freiburg with the striking sounds of its minster's tower clock; cf. SW 1, 471.

diacy of a town situated in the Mark Brandenburg amplifies the referential volume of a winter scene structured by two contrastive movements. It juxtaposes the repetitive density of snow-fall with what is perhaps a metonymical, and slightly awkward, reference to the curved rhythmical figures of ice-skating (l. 1–2 and 5–8): "Gone white the marchland town and marches | Drizzling snow did drive thee all about [. . .] | The Havelsee which thou didst stir in fleeing | Looked upon thine image in the gleaming light | The meager burden of high princely stairs | Striding in thy falling thou put down the shoe." Finally, the elaborate rhythmical tableau of Sonnet 37 renders the return to Freiburg as a paradigm for the return-structure of happiness itself (l. 1–4): "Ours the town once more will be | Returning brings each blessed joy ["Glück," happiness, CAW] | And sh all but seem like echoes of a wood | To which so many chasms lend their cry."

The urban scenographies of Benjamin's sonnets, then, showcase the temporal mode of "kairos" by translating its forms into chronotopical figurations of Heinle. His poetic alternate is either itself the author of kairotic rhythms "cut"[89] into sequences of "chronos" (nos. 11 and 38), or it is spatiotemporally co-present with their manifestations (nos. 36 and 37). In both cases, Heinle's referential relationship to each of the four sonnets is isomorphic with the "images" fusing poems and humans in Benjamin's 1928 autobiographical note. The latter tradition him and other men and women as unique crystallizations of image, voice, rhythm, gestures, and poetical verses by George. Of course, the sonnets' careful crafting of kairotic chronotopes differs considerably from the spontaneous, almost accidental emergence Benjamin ascribes to the memory-images in his retrospect. Their urban scenarios are synthetized from the *après-coup* of events

---

89   Gumbrecht, "Wozu sind Verse, Strophen und Reime gut?"

and experiences he shared with Heinle, mediating his figure through the abstracting prism of poetic stylization. With the exception of a reference to his "clustered hair" (Sonnet 38, l. 13), all individual traits of Heinle's physiognomy are notably absent. Nevertheless, the four sonnets achieve a mnemonic intensity matching that of Benjamin's retrospective elaboration of "images." Yet while the latter were actively created by his friends, with Benjamin's memory preserving them as a kind of photographic medium, the former render Heinle as an object that is "imaged" only through their verses. In them, the otherwise dominant agency of dislocation and allegorical abstraction is counterbalanced with, or even suspended by, the powerful evocation of Heinle's presence. Their chronotopes have absorbed his personal features and preserved them beyond death, just as George's poem *Gemahnt dich noch das schöne bildnis dessen* did in the 1928 retrospect. For Sonnet 11, Benjamin intensifies this process further by modelling its scenario closely on the verses of George.[90] And in the diptych of Sonnets 36 and 37, the Freiburg minster becomes the symbol of mnemonic permanence and the power of tradition, its kairotic architecture of musicalized rhythm resonating with the complex memory-sensation of Heinle. Benjamin's urban sonnets can thus be said to stage a certain paradoxical coincidence of past eventscapes and their poetic remembering. Within their circular horizons, lived experience and individual essence seem to have always-already passed into the domain of totalizing memory, just as the deathless figurations of memory seem to be always-already in the process of being traditioned without loss. Should perhaps, in other words, the task and instance of "remembrance" be always-already announcing themselves in Benjamin's sonnets?

---

90   Cf. Stefan George, "Gemahnt dich noch das schöne bildnis dessen," in Stefan George, *Das Jahr der Seele* (Stuttgart: Klett-Cotta 1982), 40.

THE PUBLISHER THANKS
PETER NOWOGRODZKI
AND PATRICK EWING,
SHEPHERDS.